ARTIFICIAL ECONOMICS

This introductory overview explores the methods, models, and interdisciplinary links of artificial economics, a new way of doing economics in which the interactions of artificial economic agents are computationally simulated to study their individual and group behavior patterns. Conceptually and intuitively, and with simple examples, Mercado addresses the differences between the basic assumptions and methods of artificial economics and those of mainstream economics. He goes on to explore various disciplines from which the concepts and methods of artificial economics originate; for example, cognitive science, neuroscience, artificial intelligence, evolutionary science, and complexity science. Introductory discussions on several controversial issues are offered, such as the application of the concepts of evolution and complexity in economics and the relationship between artificial intelligence and the philosophies of mind. This is one of the first books to fully address artificial economics, emphasizing its interdisciplinary links and presenting, in a balanced way, its occasionally controversial aspects.

Ruben Mercado is a professor at the Latin American Faculty of Social Sciences and a member of the editorial board for the journal *Computational Economics*. He holds a PhD in economics from The University of Texas at Austin. His research specializes in computational economics, economic modelling, and economic development. In the past, he has taught at the University of Texas at Austin, Bryn Mawr College, the Technological and Higher Studies Institute of Monterrey, and the Universities of Buenos Aires, Quilmes, and San Martín. He has also been a senior economist at the United Nations Development Program, a Chair for the Study of Western Hemispheric Trade at the Lozano Long Institute of Latin American Studies, and a consultant for the World Bank and the Inter-American Development Bank. He is a co-author of the pioneering textbook *Computational Economics* (2006).

Artificial Economics

Methods, Models, and Interdisciplinary Links

RUBEN MERCADO

Latin American Faculty of Social Sciences

CAMBRIDGE
UNIVERSITY PRESS

CAMBRIDGE
UNIVERSITY PRESS

University Printing House, Cambridge CB2 8BS, United Kingdom

One Liberty Plaza, 20th Floor, New York, NY 10006, USA

477 Williamstown Road, Port Melbourne, VIC 3207, Australia

314–321, 3rd Floor, Plot 3, Splendor Forum, Jasola District Centre,
New Delhi – 110025, India

103 Penang Road, #05–06/07, Visioncrest Commercial, Singapore 238467

Cambridge University Press is part of the University of Cambridge.

It furthers the University's mission by disseminating knowledge in the pursuit of
education, learning, and research at the highest international levels of excellence.

www.cambridge.org
Information on this title: www.cambridge.org/9781316517093
DOI: 10.1017/9781009036719

© Ruben Mercado 2022

First published 2022

A catalogue record for this publication is available from the British Library.

Library of Congress Cataloging-in-Publication Data
Names: Mercado, Ruben, author.
Title: Artificial economics : methods, models and interdisciplinary links / Ruben Mercado.
Description: Cambridge, United Kingdom ; New York, NY : Cambridge University Press,
2021. | Includes bibliographical references and index.
Identifiers: LCCN 2021017221 (print) | LCCN 2021017222 (ebook) | ISBN 9781316517093
(hardback) | ISBN 9781009005753 (paperback) | ISBN 9781009036719 (ebook)
Subjects: LCSH: Economics. | Economics – Mathematical models. | Artificial intelligence –
Economic aspects. | Cognitive science – Economic aspects. | BISAC: BUSINESS &
ECONOMICS / Econometrics
Classification: LCC HB71 .M565 2021 (print) | LCC HB71 (ebook) | DDC 330.1–dc23
LC record available at https://lccn.loc.gov/2021017221
LC ebook record available at https://lccn.loc.gov/2021017222

ISBN 978-1-316-51709-3 Hardback
ISBN 978-1-009-00575-3 Paperback

To

Alejandro and Graciela

Matilde and Solana

and The Family

Contents

Figures

Tables

Preface

This book presents an introductory and compact overview of methods, models, and interdisciplinary links of artificial economics. This is a new way of doing economics, in which the interactions of artificial economic agents are computationally simulated to generate and analyze their individual and group behavior patterns.

In a mostly intuitive and conceptual way, and with simple examples, the book introduces the basic assumptions and methods of artificial economics, and their differences with those of mainstream economics, the predominant paradigm in economic theory that mostly derives from neoclassical economics. The book provides basic notions of some disciplines in which several of the concepts and methods of artificial economics originate, such as cognitive science, neuroscience, artificial intelligence, evolutionary science, and the science of complexity. And the book presents introductory discussions on several controversial issues, such as the application of the concepts of evolution and complexity in economics; the relationship between artificial intelligence and the philosophies of mind; and the longstanding agent/structure problem, to which artificial economics could make some methodological and instrumental contributions.

The book addresses a broad audience, mainly but not exclusively composed of students and professionals from economics, the social sciences, computer science, and other related fields, who are curious to know about the discipline named artificial economics, and how it relates directly or indirectly to their fields of research or action.

The main text minimizes the use of mathematical expressions and presents simple illustrative examples, while matters of greater mathematical, technical, or conceptual complexity, are developed in footnotes or annexes. Also, with the intention of providing introductory coverage of the subjects addressed and a roadmap for those who want to delve into specific topics, many of the bibliographic references are made to textbooks, handbooks, and review papers.

Part I introduces the concept of the artificial agent; presents illustrative examples of models of artificial markets and artificial games, and contrasts them with similar models from mainstream economics; and discusses the methodological and instrumental differences between artificial economics and mainstream economics.

Part II addresses concepts, models, and discussions that deepen or complement topics in Part I. It introduces machine learning methods used in the field of artificial intelligence, and discusses topics related to the philosophy of mind; analyzes methods of artificial evolution, and discusses the use of the concept of evolution in economics; presents examples of models of artificial complexity, and discusses the use of concepts of the science of complexity in economics; and presents what is known as the agent/structure problem, exploring the potential contributions that could be made from artificial economics to address this problem.

Finally, the Annexes section contains specific technical or theoretical issues referred to in the main text of the book, such as the theoretical and methodological core of mainstream economics; notions on object-oriented programming; an introduction to the mathematics of static and dynamic general equilibrium models; a brief of artificial neural networks models and learning; and a presentation of the relationship between various forms of uncertainty, dynamic programming, and stochastic control.

This book is the result of my research and teaching activities in computational economics at universities in the United States, Argentina, and Mexico. Some of the topics addressed began to take shape some time ago when David A. Kendrick, Hans Amman and I wrote our *Computational Economics* textbook (Kendrick, Mercado, and Amman, 2006), while others emerged from my interdisciplinary interaction with colleagues from computer science, mathematics, physics, psychology, sociology, demography, and political science.

I thank Hans Amman and David A. Kendrick for their comments on earlier drafts of this book, for their friendship, and for so many years of shared work on teaching methods and research topics in the field of computational economics; Martín Cicowiez for his comments, and for our longstanding collaboration in the teaching and development of empirical computational models; Fernando Tohmé for his comments, for his encouragement to advance on this project, and for our discussions on computational and mathematical topics; two anonymous referees for their very valuable suggestions; Ricardo Bebczuk, Osvaldo Bodni,

Agustín Filippo, Oscar Guzmán, Facundo Malvicino, and Alejandro and Matilde Mercado, for their comments and corrections; and Silvio Waisbord for his wise strategic advising.

I also thank specially to Robert Dreesen, my commissioning editor at Cambridge University Press, for his enthusiastic and open-minded support since the reception of my book proposal, Erika Walsh, editorial assistant, for her excellent support during the preparation and publication of the book, and Grace Morris, content manager, Akash Datchinamurthy, project manager, and Ursula Acton, copyeditor, for their great work along the publication process.

Introduction

What is an artificial economy? It is a computational representation of an economic system, which allows us to simulate the interaction of artificial agents.

Artificial agents are the basic units that make up an artificial economy. These agents are computational objects containing information and rules for processing it. They can deploy very simple and silly behavior, or display sophisticated forms of artificial intelligence.

Artificial agents' characteristics and rules of behavior, their forms of interaction, and their spatial and temporal environments, are programmed and simulated computationally. From these simulations, economic structures and dynamics arise. In turn, these structures and dynamics can provoke changes in agents, affecting both their characteristics and their behavioral rules. These processes may converge, through disequilibrium situations, toward an equilibrium, or not. And they may lead to evolutionary and complex dynamics.

The methodology, assumptions and models of artificial economics (AE) contrast in at least four aspects with those of mainstream economics (ME) (a brief on the theoretical core of ME is presented in Annex B).

First, there is a contrast at the *methodological* and *instrumental* levels. ME is an essentially *mathematical* discipline, while AE is fundamentally *computational*. In ME, an economic system is usually represented by a system of equations, which in turn are obtained from the constrained optimization of functions. Therefore, the mathematical techniques of static and dynamic optimization, and static and dynamic equation systems, are among its main instruments. In AE, an economic system is programmed on a computer and its dynamic is simulated by the sequential application of its most basic rules of behavior. Thus, AE basic instruments are algorithms, software, and computer hardware.[1]

Second, there is a difference in how *individual agents* are conceptualized. ME builds its models assuming an agent endowed with *full rationality*, which acts as if it possesses a limitless capacity for gathering and processing information to maximize its well-being. This is the opposite of the artificial agent with which AE works, an agent with limited information and computational capacity and therefore with *bounded rationality*.[2]

Third, there is a contrast regarding *interactions between agents*. ME mostly assumes *global interactions*: each agent can interact simultaneously with all other agents in the economy. AE mostly works with *local interactions*: each agent only deals with other agents in its immediate environment.

Fourth, there is a difference in the *dynamics* of the economic systems being analyzed. ME tends to focus on economic *equilibrium* situations, those where the economy reaches a point at which it reproduces itself with no changes, or when it expands regularly. While AE tends to focus on the study of *disequilibrium* situations, often – although not necessarily always – evolutionary and complex.

While various aspects of the theoretical core of ME have long been questioned (e.g., criticisms coming from Marxian political economy or from Keynesian economics), in recent years there have been important developments leading to the challenge of one of its central pillars: the assumption of full rationality. This challenge comes from three new subdisciplines in economics: behavioral economics, neuroeconomics, and experimental economics. But none of these subdisciplines, so far, is a global alternative to the ME paradigm.

In this context, AE is of interest because, while for some researchers AE is complementary to ME, for others it is a globally alternative paradigm to the conventional one both in its basic concepts and its methodology. And because, like ME, it easily transcends the boundaries of economics to extend to other social disciplines such as demography, sociology, and political science. In other words, because AE may not only challenge ME

---

[1] As we will see in detail in Chapter 4, the computational nature of AE is not strictly due to its implementation on a computer, but to its algorithmic nature, which is not opposed to mathematics in general, but is linked to a special class of mathematics.

[2] It is argued that ME only assumes that an agent acts rationally if it behaves consistently: its preferences are complete and transitive, and no more than this. However, as we will see later, most typical ME models assume that agents display perfect forward-looking behavior in deterministic contexts, or rational expectations in stochastic environments.

within the economic realm, but also its "imperialist expansion" into other social sciences.[3]

There are other names that overlap with AE, depending on the methods and models used and the dynamics that emerge from simulations. According to the methods used, AE is seen as a part of the broader field of computational economics, which in turn includes computational methods to numerically solve typical ME models such as computable general equilibrium models, econometric models, and others. According to the models developed, mostly models based on agents or on cellular automata, AE is often referred to as agent-based computational economics, heterogeneous interacting agent modeling, or cellular automata based modeling. Finally, according to the type of dynamics generated, often of the evolutionary or complex type, a good deal of AE works is classified as part of the fields of evolutionary economics, and complexity economics.[4]

---

[3] "Economics imperialism" means the application of ME assumptions and methods to all or almost all areas of human behavior, including social and political actions; decisions on health, education and family; addictions; science; religion, etc. For a presentation of the concept, see Stigler (1984). For a critical discussion and appraisal, see Fine and Milonakys (2009).

[4] For information about the field of computational economics see the website of the Society for Computational Economics at http://comp-econ.org. The website www.artificial-economics.org contains information about annual AE conferences. For a broad view and for information on agent-based computational economics and on heterogeneous interacting agent modeling, see Tesfatsion and Judd (2006), Hommes and LeBaron (2018), the website created and maintained by Leigh Tesfatsion (a pioneer and great promoter of agent-based computational economics) at www2.econ.iastate.edu/tesfatsi/ace.htm, and the website of the Society for Economic Science with Heterogeneous Interacting Agents at https://sites.google.com/view/eshia-site. For introductory books to agent-based modeling, see Damaceanu (2013), Boero et al. (2015), Wilensky and Rand (2015), Hamill and Gilbert (2016), Gilbert (2019), Railsback and Grimm (2019), and Laver (2020). And for more advanced introductions, see Chen (2016) and Delli Gatti et al. (2018). For an introductory overview, and for arguments for modeling complex social dynamics with cellular automata, see Flache and Hegselmann (1998). For arguments for, and examples of, economic modeling with cellular automata, see Albin (1998). And for theory and applications (including economic ones) of cellular automata, see Him, Wu, and Li (2018). Some of the main academic journals that publish AE research are: *Journal of Artificial Societies and Social Simulation, Journal of Economic Interaction and Coordination, Computational Economics, Journal of Economic Dynamics and Control, Complexity,* and *Advances in Complex Systems.*

PART I

ARTIFICIAL ECONOMICS AND MAINSTREAM ECONOMICS

This first part introduces the concept of the artificial agent, and presents models of markets and games in which artificial agents interact. Each chapter contrasts concepts and models of AE against similar concepts and models of ME, emphasizing the differences between bounded rationality and full rationality at the agent level; between disequilibrium and equilibrium in markets and games; and between computational methods and mathematical methods.

Chapter 1, on the artificial agent, introduces the concept of the artificial agent, presents the main models of mental architectures that derive from cognitive science, and introduces some recent advances in neuroscience useful to build realistic models of artificial agents. Chapter 2, on artificial markets, presents a model of market interaction between artificial agents, and contrasts it against general static and dynamic equilibrium models typical of ME. Chapter 3, on artificial games, contrasts an artificial evolutionary game against a classic game typical of ME. Finally, Chapter 4 presents a discussion of the differences, as well as possible complementarities, between the computational methodology of AE, and the mathematical methodology of ME.

1

The Artificial Agent

The concept of *agent* has different meanings depending on the context in which it is used. In economics and in the social sciences, an agent is an individual with the capacity to act within his or her economic and social universe. More specifically, an agent is an individual who can initiate, perform, and control its actions, in order to achieve some goals.

In this chapter, we look at how the concept of economic agent developed historically within ME, and how the concept of artificial agent emerged while cognitive science became the successor of behaviorism. Then, considering that AE tries to build realistic models of artificial agents, we introduce the main models of mental architectures that derive from cognitive science, and some recent advances in neuroscience (specially within neuroeconomics, social neuroscience, and neurosociology) that relate directly to the economic and social behavior of individuals. Finally, we review some models and approaches that try to capture the cognitive, neurological, emotional, and social aspects of agents in an integrated way.

1.1 The Agent in Mainstream Economics

From the point of view of ME, an economic agent is conceived and formalized as a rational entity specialized in obtaining the greatest possible wellbeing, or utility, from each of its actions, given its preferences and the constraints within which it must operate. Specifically, an economic agent can be, for example, a consumer who, given prices of the goods she wants to consume, evaluates the quantities she could buy with her income, and chooses the best combination in order to obtain the greatest possible utility.

At the dawn of economic science, and especially from the work of utilitarian philosopher Jeremy Bentham at the end of the eighteenth century, the concept of utility was based on the seemingly obvious psychological assumption that the human being was always looking for the greatest happiness, well-being or, equivalently, the greatest amount of utility. This primitive conception regarded utility as a measurable magnitude in absolute terms and therefore comparable interpersonally, as if it were something that could be measured in the same way as the weight or height of individuals. A unit of measurement of utility, named "util," was even invented. Thus, it was assumed, for example, that from the consumption of an apple a person could obtain, say, ten utils, while, from a horseback ride, twenty utils, etc. So, one could add up the amount of utility achieved by an individual, for example, in a day, and compare it with that of another individual. The utility understood in this way is called cardinal utility.

However, as utility is a subjective magnitude, it became very difficult to sustain the claim of its interpersonal comparability. For example, two individuals can say that consuming an apple gives them great pleasure and, moreover, that on a scale of one to ten the two experience a level of pleasure or utility equal to ten. But from an objective point of view, we have no way of knowing whether a level ten effectively means the same thing to both individuals.

This inadequacy of the original concept of utility then led, from the works of John Hicks and R. G. D Allen in the 1930s, to their replacement by the concept of ordinal utility, which only requires for its construction the existence of a consistent order of individual preferences. For this conception of utility, it is only necessary for an individual to establish a preference ranking, specifying, for example, whether given two goods A and B, her preference for A is greater, equal, or less than for B, without attempting any quantitative measure, as was the case with the concept of cardinal utility.[1]

But there was still a problem, namely that such preferences, of a subjective nature, were inaccessible for direct observation. This led to Paul Samuelson's formulation of the theory of revealed preference at the end of the 1930s, which postulated that the observation of choices made by individuals reveals information about their order of preferences.[2] For example, if we observe that given two goods A and B, an individual with

---

[1] Introductions to the concepts of preferences and ordinal utility can be found nowadays in any introductory textbook to microeconomics. The first formulation of those concepts is in Hicks and Allen (1934).

[2] This theory is presented today in almost all microeconomics textbooks. The original formulation is in Samuelson (1938).

a enough income to acquire any of them, buys good A and not B, we can infer that she prefers A over B.

Samuelson's theory had a strong connection to behaviorism, a branch of psychology that was prevalent during the first half of the twentieth century. Behaviorism postulated either the nonexistence of mental phenomena or, if their existence was accepted, their inaccessibility to external observers. Therefore, it focused on the study of reactive behavior directly observable based on changes in the environment of individuals. The predominance of behaviorism – which, in the United States, lasted until the mid-twentieth century – was the intellectual and scientific environment within which Samuelson formulated the theory of revealed preference. This theory became, and remains to this day, the fundamental canon of ME to conceive and model the conduct of economic agents, without digging into their mental processes to perceive or decide. In this way, ME is as a self-contained discipline; that is, to articulate its explanations it does not need to refer to other branches of science, such as cognitive science, neuroscience, psychology, or sociology.[3]

1.2 The Agent in Artificial Economics

In the 1940s and 1950s, the main elements of an alternative paradigm to behaviorism began to gain momentum, with the pioneering works of Warren McCulloch and Walter Pitts in the field of artificial neural networks, and Alan Turing, John von Neumann, Herbert Simon, and Allen Newell in the fields of computer science and artificial intelligence. But it could be said that behaviorism begins to decline after the publication of Noam Chomsky's 1959 critical review of Burrhus F. Skinner's book *Verbal Behavior* (Skinner, 1957), then the greatest figure of behaviorism in the United States.

Contrary to behaviorism, which focused on stimulus and response functions bypassing the existence of internal representations in individuals, Chomsky demonstrated that to explain the development of language it was necessary to postulate the existence, in each individual, of a generative grammar model, that is, a set of rules that determines the grammatically correct combinations that can be made within a language. And that somehow those rules are already programmed in individuals

---

[3] For a defense of this position, see Gul and Pesendorfer (2008). For a critique, see Camerer (2008). For a discussion of mentalism versus behaviorism in economics, see Dietrich and List (2016).

from birth. Otherwise, it is impossible to explain the acquisition and development of language in children, a process whose complexity, speed, and empirical regularities greatly transcend the possibilities of conditional learning through the accumulation of experiences of stimulus and response.

This meant that in order to account for language in humans, the existence of not only internal mental representations but also of a structure of them must be recognized. In this way the rise of cognitive science began to consolidate, with an approach which postulates that by studying and modeling mental functions with methods of computer science it is possible to make verifiable inferences about the processes that take place in the mind; therefore, with a vision of mental phenomena strongly linked to the computational metaphor.[4]

In line with this paradigm, from the point of view of AE, an artificial agent is an entity capable of processing information by executing an algorithm, that is, by sequentially applying a set of rules.[5] This is no more and no less than the contemporary image of a computer. Each artificial agent has internal states and rules of conduct. Internal states are encoded into databases or data structures that contain information about agent characteristics (e.g., demographic, economic, social, cultural, etc.). While the rules of conduct are the programs (i.e., the algorithms), that encode its actions. The artificial agent takes "bits" of information from its environment, processes them to generate a representation of its world, and, given this representation, acts accordingly to achieve some goals.

In AE, an artificial agent is an artificial individual that interacts with others thus creating an artificial economy. The word *artificial* denotes here a purely algorithmic existence of agents and economies. Depending on the degree of sophistication of their behavior, different types of artificial agents can be identified. For example, Shu-Heng Cheng (2012) provides a historical review of the development of the artificial agent concept and proposes a taxonomy consisting of three categories: simple artificial agents, autonomous artificial agents, and human-like artificial agents. Simple artificial agents are those whose behavior is very elementary: for example, their behavior is always the same, or is completely random. Autonomous artificial agents are those whose behavior evolves autonomously and

---

[4] Historically, there have been several metaphors referring to the mind, such as a blank slate on which a person's experiences are recorded, a mechanical device with many gears, etc. The computational metaphor has gained prominence in recent decades and is the most used today.

[5] For a discussion of the use of the concept of agent in the social sciences, see Axtell (2000).

cannot be predicted from the initial conditions of the program that generates it, as is the case of agents built with genetic algorithms or artificial neural networks. Human-like artificial agents are those which autonomously deploy sophisticated forms of artificial intelligence, such as reinforcement learning and advanced models of decision-making under uncertainty, such as stochastic dynamic programming. Throughout the book we will see examples of these types of agents.

The various categories of artificial agents are of interest in themselves, since with them different models of artificial economies can be constructed – some that are based on very simple agents but that give rise to complex dynamics, and others that are based on sophisticated agents but yield relatively simple dynamics or, on the contrary, very complex ones. However, the category of artificial human-like agents is especially interesting because one of the main goals of AE is to have a concept of agent that contributes to, and at the same time is based on, the understanding of the behavior of real people, a goal that goes back to the origins of working with artificial agents and that was explicitly stated by pioneers of the stature of John von Neumann (1951 and 1958). Real people, in addition to possessing cognitive systems (minds) that can be interpreted as the software for information processing, have bodies of flesh and blood that can be interpreted correlatively as the hardware of such processes. And within that hardware, a fundamental part: the nervous system and, especially, the brain. When we see people in this way, we are assuming that the causal root of their behavior is in the virtual processes controlled by the software running on the brain hardware, while the body consists of input and output devices to interact with the world. Based on this characterization, to approach the goal of building realistic models of artificial agents (i.e., human-like models), AE draws mainly from two branches of modern science that relate directly to "the software and the hardware of behavior": cognitive science and neuroscience, which we will deal with in the next section. In this, AE contrasts with ME, which as we mentioned before, views itself as a self-contained behavioral science which does not need to resort to other disciplines.

1.3 Cognitive Science and Neuroscience

1.3.1 Cognitive Science

From the point of view of cognitive science, thought can be understood in terms of the existence of representational structures in the mind, and computational processes that operate on those structures. Thus, the mind is seen as an information processor.[6] There are several models that attempt to capture the way mental processes of representation and computing occur, but there are currently two main approaches to the functional architecture of the mind.[7]

The first one, predominant in classical cognitive science, is the rules-based architecture, whose founding fathers include Noam Chomsky, Allen Newell, and Herbert Simon and where Jerry Fodor, Marvin Minsky, and others have later stood out. This approach sees the mind as if it were a conventional computer that processes symbols sequentially using "if-then" rules and procedures that operate on them.

For example, consider the representation of thoughts about the economies of countries. When we think about such economies, we can represent them with concepts such as advanced or backward, innovative or traditional, productive or unproductive, with high or low investment, growing or stagnant, etc., and we can operate on such representations with rules such as:

a. If E is a productive economy, then E is an advanced economy
b. If E wants to be an advanced economy, then E must be innovative
c. If E is a backward economy, then E is a low-investment economy

From a database containing numerous such rules, we can make inferences that result in specific behaviors. A simple case would be:

a. E wants to be an advanced economy
b. If E wants to be an advanced economy, then E must be innovative
c. Therefore, E must be innovative

In short, a rule-based functional architecture has representational structures and operates on them (in a way, it reasons) by means of chains of rules. These operations can be complemented by efficient procedures to bring rules from memory without having to review all of them each time an inference is made; to resolve conflicts between rules; and to learn new rules,

---

[6] For systematic introductions to cognitive science, see Thagard (2005), which is organized by modes of mental representation, Friedenberg and Silverman (2011), which is organized by subdisciplines, and Bermúdez (2014), which is organized around theories and problems. For comprehensive cognitive science coverage, see Frankish and Ramsey (2012) and Wilson and Keil (2001). For a comprehensive presentation of computational cognitive modeling, also known as computational psychology, see Sun (2008).

[7] For a more extended and deeper presentation of mental architectures along the lines briefly introduced in this section, see Thagard (2012).

either by accumulation of experience or by combining existing rules into a new one. For example, if we have the following rules:

a. If E is a productive economy, then E is an advanced economy
b. If E is an advanced economy, then E is a growing economy

we can generate a new rule such as:

c. If E is a productive economy, then E is a growing economy

The second main approach to the functional architecture of the mind is connectionism, among whose founding fathers are Warren McCulloch and Walter Pitts, and where Patricia Churchland, Paul Churchland, and others, have since stood out. This approach sees the functioning of the mind as an artificial neural network that performs a multitude of parallel processing, that is, in a simultaneous way, with a very general and highly plastic basic structure that reconfigures itself through learning. In this approximation, information is not encoded in rules, but through connections between nodes that are neuron-like mini processors.

An example analogous to the one seen previously can be represented in an artificial neural network like the one in Figure 1.1. In this network, each

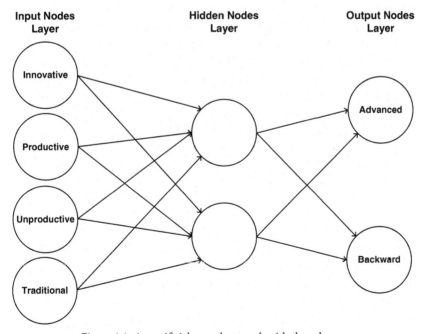

Figure 1.1 An artificial neural network with three layers

input and output node contains a concept. The links between nodes can be positive or negative, in a similar way that neurons in the brain are connected by synapses that allow one to excite or inhibit others.

We see that in this example there is a network of three layers: one input layer, which receives the data fed into the network; one output layer, which contains the results or predictions generated by the network; and one (which could be more than one) hidden layer. The hidden layer contains nodes without a specific conceptual interpretation, and whose function is to help provide a statistical connection between inputs and outputs, difficult to express in words or to represent by rules. These nodes are elementary units of data processing. They react to the input stimuli by firing stimuli toward the output nodes. Later, in Chapter 5 and in Annex D, we'll look at more details about neural networks.

Notice that in the classical cognitive science approach just discussed, rules connect input concepts and generate one output concept. While in the connectionist approach, the output layer of an artificial neural network may contain more than one concept, and there is not a single rule connecting input and output layers, but a set of connection patterns spanning the nodes of the three layers. Also, in an artificial neural network a node does not necessarily constitute a representative or symbolic unit, such as a concept. That role can be fulfilled by a subnet of nodes.

The main differences between the classical and the connectionist approaches can then be thought of as the first one emphasizing the sequential manipulation of symbolic objects according to logical or algebraic rules, and the second one emphasizing the manipulation in parallel – that is, simultaneously – of sub-symbolic objects according to interconnection patterns.[8]

From what we said so far, the modeling of artificial agents in AE is mostly linked to the approximation of classical cognitive science. That is, agents are sequential rule processors. Although nothing prevents them from being modeled with methods linked to connectionism (i.e., providing each agent with an artificial neural network), although so far this practice is a minority.

1.3.2 Neuroscience

Just as cognitive science received a strong boost from the development of artificial intelligence from the 1950s onwards, at the same time neuroscience accelerated its development thanks to advances in other disciplines

---

[8] Although it should be noted that in principle a sequential processor based on rules can simulate any parallel processing.

such as molecular biology, electrophysiology, and computational neuroscience. Of interest to AE are advances in cognitive neuroscience, which studies the relationship between states and mental functions, and neural circuits. Recent developments have been made in this field due to the introduction of noninvasive instruments that allow the scanning of the living brain, such as functional magnetic resonance imaging, positron emission tomography, computed tomography by single photon emission, and other techniques. These new instruments have made it possible to advance the understanding of the structure and dynamics of areas, hierarchies, and brain circuits, and their relationship with cognitive and emotional phenomena.

Important developments concerning the neural basis of decision-making took place in the mid-1980s and the mid-1990s (Damasio, 2009). Individuals who suffered bilateral brain damage in the ventral and middle ventral sector of the prefrontal cortex showed emotional problems, such as decreased emotional resonance, or lack of social emotions such as compassion or shame. They also showed significant flaws in their decision-making, especially in decisions related to economic and social relations: individuals decided against their interests, and against the interests of their closest people, despite not manifesting problems of logical reasoning, learning, memory, language, or perception. This led to the neuroscientific study of the role of emotions in decision-making (in making the right decisions, and not just in making the wrong ones, as previously believed) a field in which figures such as Antonio Damasio stand out.[9] The problems identified in economic and social decisions boosted the development of new disciplines: neuroeconomics, social neuroscience and neurosociology.

Neuroeconomics, a field with leading figures such as Paul Glimcher, Ernst Fehr, and Colin Camerer, studies the neural foundations of valuation-based decision-making processes.[10] Since economics emphasizes the role of cost/benefit analysis in individual decision-making, the study of neural processes that are at the basis of valuation processes has been, unsurprisingly, one of the central themes of neuroeconomics.

Some leading neuroeconomists propose a sequence of five steps to characterize the structure of processes of decision-making (Rangel, Camerer, and Montague, 2008). In the first step, the agent builds a representation of the problem on which to decide, where such

---

[9] For an enjoyable and comprehensive introduction to this theme, see Damasio (2005).

[10] For a comprehensive introduction to and presentation of neuroeconomics, see Glimcher and Fehr (2014).

representation includes the analysis of its internal state, the external states, and its possible actions. In the case of an animal, for example, it can identify its internal state (hunger), the external state (existence of a prey), and its possible actions (chasing the prey or not). In the second step, values are assigned to possible actions, based on internal or external states. For example, if the internal state is "very hungry," and there is a prey in the vicinity, the action of going out to pursue it will have a higher value than not to go out. In the third step, considering those valuations, the action whose relative value is the highest is chosen. In the fourth step, it is assessed how desirable the result of the chosen action was. For example, whether the trapped prey proved a satisfactory food or not. Finally, in the fifth step, the previous steps are updated in a learning process with the aim of improving future decisions.

As can be inferred from this, we should note that neuroeconomics is used to study the neural bases of decision-making not only in humans, but also in animals. And that, although some experiments are carried out on humans, many are done with animals.

In what follows, we will mention some highlights of research in neuroeconomics. Let's start with the field of decision-making under uncertainty, that is, when there is an action that does not always generate the same result, but can yield alternative results, each of which has a probability of occurrence. In this case, the role of the neurotransmitter dopamine in the transmission of uncertainty information through the cerebral cortex is highlighted. Dopamine levels increase when the level of uncertainty that individuals face when deciding also increases. For example, if the expected result of an action occurs, dopamine levels do not increase. However, the opposite occurs when the expected result of an action does not occur, increasing the activity of dopamine-producing neurons. Also related to the process of decision-making under uncertainty, there is evidence that neurons in the left parietal circuits of the brain encode information on the probability of the effects of decisions, and on their relative value. This is interpreted as those neurons encoding the expected utility of decisions (i.e., the weighted average of the utilities of each of the possible outcomes).

Another finding relates to time preference, the relative value that individuals give to the present with respect to the future. This happens, for example, when a person puts more value on the fact of consuming a glass of wine today, than doing it within a week. This may lead to this person requiring compensation to defer present consumption, demanding, for example, two glasses of wine within a week in exchange for one today. There are laboratory findings that indicate that the neurotransmitter serotonin plays a role in modulating time preference. A higher serotonin level makes the relative value of a good in the future smaller than its value in the present. That is to say that it could lead, for example, to a person to ask for three glasses of wine instead of two within a week, to compensate for not consuming one glass in the present.

For some researchers such as Paul Glimcher (2003), neuroeconomics also provides an explanation and a methodology for addressing the existence and function of neural circuits and organs. From this approach, which in turn is largely based on the pioneering work of neuroscientist David Marr, neural circuits and organs are solutions to optimization problems, derived from the need to maximize the evolutionary adaptation of the organism. The nervous system would function to make decisions under uncertainty to ultimately ensure the survival and reproduction of individuals and the species. Therefore, to understand a behavior and its mental and neural bases, we should start asking what the overall goal of the behavior is, and then determining what its cognitive representations and optimal neural implementations would be. This approach is presented as a better alternative to the standard "reflexological" approach to neuroscience, which is seen as focused on the study of very simple goal-oriented behaviors.

Social neuroscience and neurosociology are two disciplines that have undergone accelerated development in recent years. Social neuroscience, a field with researchers such as John Cacioppo and Gary Berntson, studies how biological organisms implement social behaviors and processes through neural, neuroendocrine, immune, and metabolic mechanisms, warning that neural representations of social interaction do not reside in any singular neural structure, and that the neurochemistry that mediates such interaction is also diverse (Norman et al., 2013). However, attention has been paid to the role of oxytocin (a hormone produced in the cerebral hypothalamus that is released into the bloodstream through the pituitary gland) in the social behavior of humans. Such a hormone would play an important role in modulating social perception, social knowledge, and social behavior, and therefore in promoting social approximation and affiliation between individuals.

Neurosociology, a discipline with figures such as David Franks and Warren TenHouten, studies the influence of society on the mind, and the influence of the mind on neural microstructures, something particularly significant in the early stages of individual development. The starting point of this discipline is the postulate that human beings do not relate directly to their environment, but do so through social and cultural filters and, moreover, that cultural practices and social categories are transmitted through interaction with other human beings.[11] Among the most significant recent discoveries for neurosociology are mirror neurons. As we observe someone performing an action or expressing a feeling, these neurons are activated and give rise to a process of internal imitation of such behavior. Mirror neurons would be at the basis of empathetic behaviors and the possibility of "reading the mind" of others or putting themselves in the role of others, by internally simulating behaviors, thoughts, and emotional states of their own and others. In this way, people would "perform" in their motor cerebral cortex those behaviors they observe in others. Another significant finding is that the part of the brain called the amygdala, the center of feelings of fear and anger in all mammals and reptiles, would be involved in the dynamics of social status. The more individuals seek to establish their superiority over others, the more fear and anger in the amygdala are activated.

Other suggestive findings have to do with the fact that the brains of various social animals would be attuned to the frequencies that are important for communication and social behavior, leading to the description of the nervous system of several mammals, even humans, as a social brain. Participants in a process of social interaction are continuously active, modifying their actions in response to the changing actions of those with whom they are interacting. This results in interactional synchrony. How the brains of participants in social interaction work during this process is a matter of recent research, facilitated by techniques such as hyperscanning, a method by which several individuals, each in a resonance imaging device, interact while their brains are scanned simultaneously. Some studies show that there is synchronization of certain rhythms of brain functioning during processes of social interaction, whether verbal or nonverbal in nature. Moreover, Michael Tomasello claims that networked minds implement distributed processes of intentionality and awareness. Although here it is important to distinguish between the processes of coordination of behaviors, which many animals implement and which are not based on strategic thinking but only on their individual selfishness, and collaborative behaviors, which are based on the strategic thinking of individuals and empathetic processes among them (Tomasello, 2014).

A particularly important point in relation to the formation and maintenance of social interactions is the fact that humans are evolved apes, and

---

[11] For a compact presentation of neurosociology, see Franks (2019). For an encompassing presentation, see Franks and Turner (2013).

apes are animals that, unlike others which are biologically programmed to form groups and societies (such as bees or ants), have weak ties and are not very social. Similarly, humans form and undo groups in an ongoing process of fusion and fission. For some researchers it is because of this that we have a broad set of emotions, anchored in the subcortical areas of our brain, which play a fundamental role for our socialization. Emotional energy would be the glue that allows us to create bonds, solidarity, and commitments, for group formation. But because group formation depends on positive emotions, and we also have many negatives ones, we need culture (norms, beliefs, and values), moral sanctions, and emotions such as guilt and shame, to keep episodes of breakdown of social interaction in line (Massey, 2002; Stets and Turner, 2006; Turner and Maryanski, 2013).

1.4 Emotion, Reason, and Social Links: Integrated Agents

We have seen how cognitive science and neuroscience address the cognitive, neurological, emotional, and social aspects of individuals. In this section, we will present an approximation due to Joshua Epstein that seeks to articulate these aspects in a model of an integrated artificial agent. And then we will present two approaches (*embodied and embedded* cognitive science, and the Freudian mental model) that go beyond the typical fields of conventional cognitive science and neuroscience and that could also be useful for advancing in the modeling of integrated artificial agents.

Joshua Epstein proposed an integrated artificial agent model which he calls *Agent_Zero* (Epstein, 2013). Epstein's starting point is that emotional, cognitive, and social factors shape the behavior of individuals and groups, and are therefore at the heart of the deployment of social and economic dynamics, such as financial panics. *Agent_Zero* has three modules that interact with each other: the emotional/affective module; the cognitive/ deliberative module; and the social module, this one characterized by network/contagion effects.

The observed behavior of such an agent results from the interconnection between its three modules, which generates a disposition to act. This disposition is a very simple mathematical function – just the sum – of indicators corresponding to each of the three modules, which generates a number. If that number exceeds some threshold, the agent acts. Otherwise, it doesn't. Therefore, the actions of the agent are binary: buy a car or not, marry or not, participate in a collective protest or not, etc.

The emotional/affective module is conceived as a Pavlovian theory of associative learning. More precisely, it is a generalization of what is known as Rescorla–Wagner conditioning model, a model widely used in experimental psychology. This model captures some simple features of learning processes (e.g., fear conditioning), such as an organism learning when some unexpected events violate its expectations. The adaptation or change in expectations depends on the difference between the observed and expected values. Thus, the learning process is fast at first, then slowly approaching the observed values.

In the cognitive/deliberative module, agents compute probabilities of event occurrences based on local samples of observations (which come to them as stimuli) from a dynamic environment. Since agents are supposed to have bounded rationality, the probabilities they compute can be skewed.

For the social module, a network transmission model (or contagion model) is used, although it is not a typical model of contagion by imitation of the observed behavior of other agents, since what is spread are the dispositions to act. In other words, the dispositions to act of other agents are variables within the function of an agent's disposition to act, something of which the agent may not be aware. Thus, the contagion process within a network of agents can be unconscious.

Agent_Zero is not a model of mental or brain areas. Rather, it is a proposal for abstract synthesis of contents of neuroscience, cognitive science, and the social sciences that aims to model the behavior of individuals within groups, using as inputs the advances in such sciences. In other words, it is a simple synthetic model that purports to include a representation of the interrelationship between passions, reason (bounded or imperfect), and social influence, and to generate behaviors that result from such interrelationship.

Finally, we will present basic notions about *embodied and embedded* cognitive science, and about the Freudian mental model, both of which, as we mentioned, could also be useful for advancing in the modeling of integrated agents.

In relatively recent times has developed a branch of cognitive science known as *embodied and embedded*.[12] It emphasizes that cognitive processes are not abstract but occur in the dynamic interaction of systems with bodies that are embedded in a physical and social environment. Thus, a proper model of an agent should consider its cognitive processes as inseparable from its body and its body as inseparable from the environment. For some

---

[12] For a wide coverage of this approach, see Calvo and Gomila (2008).

researchers, this approach rejects, and for others restricts, the vision of mainstream cognitive science (both in its classical and connectionist branches) about an agent as a processor of information that manipulates abstract representations, whether symbolic or sub-symbolic. While for others it is complementary to mainstream cognitive science.

The *embodied and embedded* vision posits that mental or cognitive processes are strongly influenced by the states of the body and by the physical and social environment. Regarding *embodiment*, it is held that the internal states of the body (hormonal and homeostatic) probably through the emotional system, strongly influence mental states, that is, the kind of cognitive processes that emerge in the brain. As for *embeddedness*, it is postulated that the physical interaction between body and environment constrains the behaviors of the organism, and that the environment influences and partly constitutes the cognitive processes that emerge from the interaction with the world.

It has usually been considered that mental processes can be separated between high-level processes (cognitive processes related to symbolic manipulation, planning, and strategic thinking), and sensory and motor processes without a decisive influence on the former. What this approach holds is that the influence of sensory and motor processes on cognitive processes is decisive or, even more, that the division between one and the other is impossible. And that the appropriate approach is the scientific study of neural, bodily, and environmental factors, interacting in real time.

As another useful approach for the construction of an integrated agent model, we can mention the well-known Freudian mental model, which is at the root of psychoanalysis. Already at the beginning of the twentieth century, Sigmund Freud developed a model that tried to articulate mental phenomena in an integrated way with its biological basis and with its social environment.[13] In this model, and speaking very schematically, the impulses and drives emanating from the biological substrate of the individual emerge in the human psyche through the id (the unconscious), while the moral social restrictions are present through the super-ego. Thus, the ego is permanently in an arbiter position between those two conditioning factors or forces that harass it. The dynamic interaction between these three

---

[13] For an introduction to the historical development and to the structures of Freud's models of mind, see Sandler et al. (1997). As Freud postulated the existence of structured mental phenomena, it could be said that he was ahead of cognitive science by almost six decades, since that science, as we saw earlier, emerged in the late 1950s after the predominance of behaviorism – which denied or ruled out the modeling of mental phenomena – that began with John Watson in the 1920s and reached its apex with Burrhus F. Skinner in the 1950s.

elements (id, ego and super-ego) results in the deployment of strong intra-psychic conflicts that cause ambivalent behaviors, denial and parapraxis (such as slips of the tongue), and various types of pathologies (hysteria, neurosis, psychosis), issues that are usually not addressed in the modeling of artificial agents.[14]

Even though for most psychoanalysts psychoanalysis has a somehow autonomous existence and is qualitatively distinct from cognitive science, neuroscience, and artificial intelligence, over time some bridges have been built with these disciplines as evidenced, for example, by the work of Nobel laureate Eric Kandel (2005), Mark Solms, and other neuroscientists, who gave rise to what is now known as neuropsychoanalysis (Solms and Turnbull, 2011); by Wilma Bucci's contributions to linking psychoanalysis and cognitive science (Bucci, 1997; van Nuys, 2010); and by some early works trying to connect psychoanalysis and artificial intelligence (Turkle, 1988; Rodado and Rendon, 1996). This also applies in some recent developments in the field of artificial intelligence that use and implement psychoanalytical ideas (Dietrich et al., 2009), as, for example, the application of the Freudian concept of defense mechanisms in the modeling of multi-agent cognitive systems (Gelbard, 2017), and the development of a model of the brain on the basis of psychoanalytical ideas together with the theoretical computer science concept of layered model, with a top layer referring to the Freudian model of the psyche, beneath which lies a layer of neuro-symbolism, beneath which lies the hardware or purely physically described part of the system (Brandstätter et al., 2015).

In this chapter, we presented the basic characteristics of artificial agents considered individually. Now it's time to move to the analysis of the interactions between agents. That is, to the building of artificial economies. In the next two chapters we will present, for illustrative purposes, some models that are very useful for getting into the functioning of artificial economies. At the same time, we will highlight the differences in the way economic phenomena are addressed by AE as opposed to ME. In Chapter 2, we will introduce a famous AE model known as Sugarscape, and then we will contrast it with general equilibrium models typical of ME. In Chapter 3, we will introduce a classic game of game theory known as the prisoner's dilemma, and we will contrast it with an artificial evolutionary game based on the same dilemma.

---

[14] Although it is worth mentioning that the approach of mental problems and illnesses from an artificial intelligence perspective is now done within the relatively new field known as computational psychiatry. For an introduction to this topic, see Huys, Maia, and Frank (2016).

2

Artificial Markets

In the previous chapter we focused on the characteristics of artificial agents. In this chapter, we'll start looking at some of their forms of interaction. First, we will introduce two versions of the famous Sugarscape model developed by Joshua Epstein and Robert Axtell (Epstein and Axtell, 1996), which is an excellent model for getting into AE. In the first version, artificial agents are very simple and dedicated, in an environment in which there is only one resource called sugar, to collect and consume that resource to meet their metabolic needs. In the second version, the environment provides two resources, sugar and spice. And the artificial agents are more sophisticated, as they are not only dedicated to collecting and consuming such resources but also engage into market exchanges of them. Finally, we present a static and a dynamic model of market economies, typical of ME, in a way that illustrates by contrast the assumptions of AE versus the ones of ME.

2.1 A Model of Artificial Economics with Movement

Let's start with the first version of our artificial economy: a Sugarscape model with movement. Suppose that artificial agents are distributed in a space or geography that has the shape of a grid in which each cell is occupied by some quantity of a resource called sugar.

Figure 2.1 shows a grid of 50 × 50 cells, with two peaks of sugar, one in the northeast area and one in the southwest.[1] The color intensity denotes the

---

[1] Although the Sugarscape grid is represented in the text as a square and flat surface, actually it is what is geometrically known as the surface of a Torus (a geometrical object that has the shape of a donut). Therefore, the cells at the upper and lower ends, and at the left and right ends are adjacent.

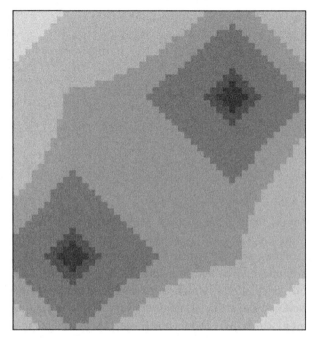

Figure 2.1 A Sugarscape grid with two peaks

quantity of sugar in each cell: the darker, the more sugar. The closer we get to the peaks, the more sugar there is. The farther, the less. Each agent collects and consumes the quantity of sugar available in the cell in which is located, and at the end of each period that quantity returns to its initial level. Thus, we can think of the grid as a natural environment that regenerates itself.[2]

Suppose that each agent can live indefinitely if it meets some minimum metabolic needs, that is, in order not to die it must consume a given quantity of sugar in each period. Suppose also that each agent has a range of vision of its environment, which allows it to see only in four directions (north, south, east, and west), and only up to a given distance. Each agent will be able to move, in each period, only within the neighborhood covered by its range of vision.

Figure 2.2 shows, as shaded cells, the neighborhood of an agent with a vision range equal to three, while the agent is represented by a black cell.

---

[2] Such a grid is an extremely simple case of what's known as a cellular automaton where each cell, at the end of each period, returns to its initial state. In Chapter 7, we will present an introduction to cellular automata.

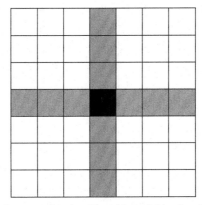

Figure 2.2 An agent (black cell) and its neighborhood (grey cells)

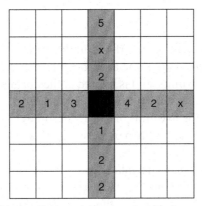

Figure 2.3 An agent (black cell) in a neighborhood with other agents (x), and cells with different quantities of sugar available

Metabolism and vision range can be thought of as the genetic code of the agent. Now let's define a rule of conduct for agents, which is a movement rule. In each period, each agent explores its neighborhood by searching for the free cell with the highest quantity of sugar. When it finds that cell, it moves to it, adds to its stock the quantity of sugar found, and subtracts what it needs to consume to satisfy its metabolism.

For example, suppose the agent has, as in the aforementioned example, a vision range equal to three and a metabolism equal to two, that is, to survive in each period it needs to consume two units of sugar. Suppose that the agent is in the neighborhood shown in Figure 2.3, where the numbers in each cell indicate the quantity of sugar, and where the cells with an x mean they are occupied by another agent.

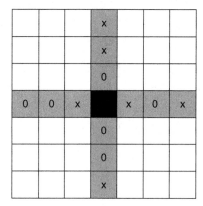

Figure 2.4 An agent (black cell) in a neighborhood with other agents (x) and zero sugar available

The agent explores its neighborhood in the north, south, east, and west directions, and discovers that the available cell with the most sugar is the one that contains five units, and is located at the northern end of its vision range. That is, three cells up from its current position. Therefore, it moves to that cell, collects the five units of sugar, consumes two, and accumulates three. Suppose now that, in the next period, the agent is in a situation like the one depicted in Figure 2.4.

In this case, all cells in its neighborhood are occupied by other agents, or are unoccupied, but do not contain sugar. As our agent accumulated a stock of three units of sugar in the previous period, stays where it is, and consumes the necessary sugar according to its metabolic need (i.e., two units), keeping a stock of one unit.

Let's finally assume that in the next period our agent is in an identical situation to the previous one. In such a case, its sugar stock won't be enough to satisfy its metabolism, and it will not have a chance of increasing it by moving to any cell within its neighborhood. Therefore, it will die, thereby disappearing from the Sugarscape.

More interesting than analyzing the behavior and life cycle of an isolated agent is to study what happens in a universe in which many agents live. We can guess that the study of this type of problem is quite complicated when compared to the simple individual examples that we have just presented, and that we solved almost intuitively. Indeed, to study a multi-agent universe we need to use more powerful and sophisticated tools, such as computational simulations in which we run programs containing all the

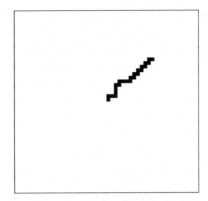

Figure 2.5 An agent moving through the Sugarscape

information about artificial agents: their characteristics, their rules of individual behavior and of interaction with others, and the environment in which they live.

The computational implementation of a model like the one we are dealing with can be done with standard programming methods, or by object-oriented programming techniques and software, a highly structured way of building computational objects encapsulated in themselves, but with the capacity of interacting with others. Notions about this type of programming are presented in Annex A.

Before we turn to the analysis of the evolution of a population of many artificial agents, let us perform a first and simple computational simulation. Suppose we have only one agent, whose starting position is at the midpoint of the 50 × 50 cell grid that contains, as we have seen, the geography of the available sugar. Let's also assume that the agent's metabolism is equal to one, and its vision range equal to one. Figure 2.5 shows the agent's journey (black cells) over the grid for a simulation spanning fifty periods. The agent begins in the center of the grid, in a valley with relatively little sugar and, unsurprisingly, moves in the direction of one of the peaks where the most sugar is concentrated: in this case, toward the peak in the northeast area of the grid. It reaches the peak after twenty-three displacements. Once there, it no longer moves, and stays to live in that position indefinitely.

Now, let's perform the simulation of the evolution of a large population of artificial agents. To do this we begin by generating an initial population of 721 agents randomly distributed over the geography of the Sugarscape. For each agent we generate random values distributed between one and five units of sugar, which will be the values of their minimum metabolic need for subsistence. That is to say that some agents will be able to survive by consuming only one unit of sugar, others two, others three, others four, and others five. Also, we randomly generate values between one and five for the vision range of each agent, that is that there will be agents that can only see and move in a one-cell neighborhood, others in a two-cell neighborhood, and so on, up to a maximum of five cells.

We performed a simulation consisting of six periods (or runs). In each period, agents act according to their rule of behavior, that is, moving, collecting, and consuming sugar.

Figure 2.6 shows the spatial distribution of artificial agents (in black color) in the Sugarscape in each of the six periods.[3]

In the first period (panel a) the population of artificial agents is approximately evenly distributed over the grid. However, as time passes, the population declines: from 721 agents in the first period to 436 in the second (panel b), 371 in the third (panel c), and so on, due to the death of those who do not have enough sugar to meet their minimum metabolic needs. We can see how survivors tend, as one would expect, to migrate and cluster around the sugar peaks found in the northeast and southwest areas of the grid, where the survival conditions are most favorable. Finally, the population stabilizes both in number (with approximately 342 agents) and in its location (in the two areas of the grid with the highest sugar density).

Here we have assumed that the Sugarscape grid could be thought of as a natural environment that regenerates autonomously: in each period each cell refills with the same quantity of sugar that it had in the initial period. This explains why the agent population ends up in a stable situation. Otherwise, if the sugar level of each cell was not automatically replenished, agents would completely exhaust their environment, and eventually they would all die.

In addition to analyzing the degree of survival and spatial behavior of the population of agents, we can compute other interesting statistics that reflect the evolutionary dynamic of the Sugarscape. For example, in each period we can add, on the one hand, the metabolism levels of all agents and, on the other, their vision ranges, and divide them by the number of living agents, to obtain the average metabolism and average vision of the population. If we do that for the simulation we just performed, we see that the average level of population metabolism goes from a value of 3.01 units of sugar in the initial period to a value of 2.07 units in the final period. While

---

[3] For a computational implementation in MATLAB and a simulation of this version of the Sugarscape with different parameter values, see Kendrick, Mercado, and Amman (2006), pp. 267–290.

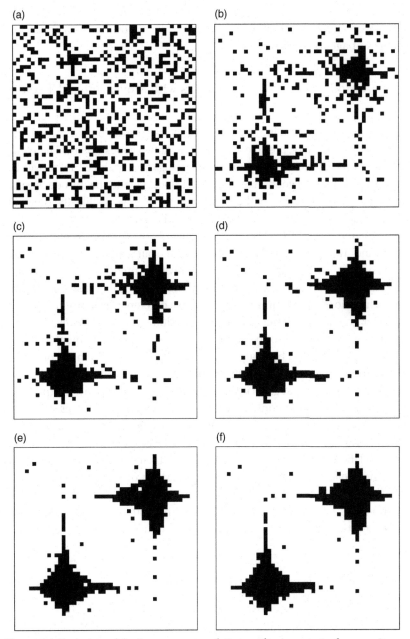

Figure 2.6 Evolution of the Sugarscape population, with movement rule, over six periods

the average vision level ranges from 3.01 to 3.18. In other words, as one would expect, lower metabolic needs and wider vision ranges increase the chances of agents' survival.

2.2 A Model of Artificial Economics with Movement and Trade

We will now present a model that extends the previous one, allowing agents to trade goods. Thus, we are introducing an economic institution: the market. For market exchanges to be possible, we need at least two goods to exist. Therefore, we add to the model a new good: besides sugar, in each cell there will be a quantity of another good that we will call spice. Due to the introduction of a new good, the geography of the Sugarscape will change. Unlike the previous model, where we had two sugar peaks, we will now have two peaks in the northeast and southwest areas where the quantity of sugar predominates over spice, and two peaks in the northwest and southeast areas where spice predominates over sugar. As in the previous model, each agent has a metabolism and a range of vision and can move, in each period, only within its neighborhood. We assume that agents have different preferences for one or the other good, which results in each agent valuing them differently.

Let's define two rules of behavior for agents: one of movement and one of exchange. Let's start by analyzing the movement rule. As in the previous model, in each period, each agent explores its neighborhood by looking for the nearest free cell that gives it the greatest well-being, that is, the quantity of sugar and spice that contributes most to meet its preferences. When it finds that cell, it moves to it, and collects all the goods found there.

What will agents' preferences depend on? We can assume that they depend on the relationship, at any given time, between their stock of sugar relative to their metabolic need for sugar, versus their stock of spice relative to their metabolic need for spice. For example, an agent with little sugar in stock relative to its need for sugar consumption, and with a lot of spice in stock relative to its need for spice consumption, will value more sugar over spice.[4]

---

[4] Mathematically, in this version of the Sugarscape model, each agent's preferences are represented by a welfare function W of the following form, known as a Cobb–Douglass-type function:

$$W(w_{su}, w_{sp}) = w_{su}^{m_{su}/m_T} w_{sp}^{m_{sp}/m_T}$$

where w_{su} is the quantity of sugar in the agent's stock, w_{sp} is its stock of spice, m_{su} is its metabolic need for sugar, and m_{sp} its metabolic need for spice, and where $m_T = m_{su} + m_{sp}$. The arguments of the welfare function are accumulated stocks, so the

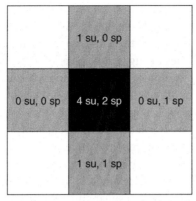

Figure 2.7 Distribution of sugar (su) and spice (sp) in possession of an agent (black cell), and in its neighborhood (grey cells)

Figure 2.7 shows the situation of an agent with a vision range equal to one, who explores its neighborhood in search of the free cell that gives it the greatest well-being. Suppose the agent has a metabolic need of three units of sugar and three of spice. And that counts in stock with four units of sugar and two of spice. Therefore, given its situation at this time, the agent will value spice more than sugar. Suppose the quantities of sugar and spice in each cell of its neighborhood are the ones shown in Figure 2.7, where su indicates sugar and sp spice. And that the agent begins its exploration from the cell on the left and continues in the clockwise direction.

The first cell (the west cell) will not be particularly attractive to the agent, as it contains neither sugar nor spice. Therefore, it will prefer the second (the northern one) as it has at least one unit of sugar. However, given its metabolic needs, the agent urgently needs to get at least one spice unit so as not to die. Thus, it will prefer the third cell (the eastern one). Finally, since the last cell (the southern one) contains one unit of sugar and one of spice, it will be the preferred one, as it will be the one that provides the greatest well-being. So, the agent will move to it, add one unit of sugar to its stock of four units, and one unit of spice to its stock of two units, and consume three units of each (which will allow it to continue alive), thus finally left in its stock two units sugar and none of spice.[5]

---

welfare is state dependent. This is an appropriate way to represent a situation in which agents do not consume all their stocks within a period.

[5] If we use the agent's welfare function to compute the well-being derived from moving to each of the cells in the agent's neighborhood according to the numerical example presented in the text, we have for the east cell W = 2.82, for the north W = 3.13, for the west W = 3.46, and for the south W = 3.87.

Now let's move on to the analysis of the trade rule. Once in its new cell, the agent will be able to exchange goods with its neighbors. It will do this based on its preferences, and therefore on its own valuations regarding having specific quantities of sugar and spice.[6]

For example, if agent A has 4 kg of spice and a metabolic need of 2 kg of spice, and also has 1 kg of sugar and a metabolic need of 2 kg of sugar, it will feel rich in spice and poor in sugar. This means that it will value sugar more than spice, and therefore it will be a buyer of sugar at a relatively high price, and a seller of spice at a relatively low price.

On the other hand, if its neighbor agent B has 1 kg of spice and a metabolic need of 2 kg of spice and 4 kg of sugar, and a metabolic need of 2 kg of sugar, it will feel rich in sugar and poor in spice. Then it will value spice more than sugar, and it will be a spice buyer at a relatively high price, and a sugar seller at a relatively low price.

Therefore, if agent A and its neighbor B meet to make an exchange, agent A will surely be a sugar buyer and a seller of spice, while B will be a sugar seller and a spice buyer. But what will be the relative price of sugar in terms of spice to which they will exchange? Obviously, it must be a price that satisfies both the seller and the buyer. The price must then be less than the maximum price at which agent A is willing to buy sugar, and higher than the minimum price at which agent B is willing to sell sugar.

Of all possible prices in the range between that maximum and minimum, what will be the price at which A and B exchange sugar and spice? We will assume that both agents perform a bilateral bargaining process. They agree on a price falling within the interval between those maximum and minimum prices, and as a function of that price they determine the quantities to exchange.[7] The exchange takes place only if it is mutually

---

[6] According to ME microeconomic theory, an agent's valuation of each good is determined by the marginal rate of substitution (MRS) of one good for another. In our case, given the welfare function W we are using, the MRS of spice per one unit of sugar is:

$$\text{MRS} = \frac{\partial W(w_{su}, w_{sp})}{\partial w_{su}} \bigg/ \frac{\partial W(w_{su}, w_{sp})}{\partial w_{sp}} = \frac{W_{sp}}{m_{sp}} \bigg/ \frac{W_{su}}{m_{su}}$$

The direction that the exchange takes between each pair of agents is as follows: spice goes from the agent with a higher MRS to the agent with a lower MRS, while sugar moves in the opposite direction.

[7] For the determination of the exchange price, there are many possible rules for the bargaining process. In the Sugarscape model we are dealing with, and following Epstein and Axtell (1996), the relative price p is determined as the geometric mean of the marginal rate of substitution (MRS) of agents A and B:

satisfactory, that is, if it increases both agents' welfare. This process repeats until both agents' welfare cannot be increased anymore through trade.[8]

A similar bilateral bargaining process will take place with each of the agents within agent A's neighborhood, in which different quantities of goods will be offered and demanded at different prices. Finally, in each period, agent A will accumulate goods according to the quantities it collected in the Sugarscape plus those exchanged with its neighbors, and will reduce its stocks according to what it needs to consume given its metabolic needs of sugar and spice. A similar process will be repeated for each of the Sugarscape agents.

For what we have seen so far, we can conclude that the agent we are dealing with is quite like a typical ME agent: it has stable and well-defined preferences and acts rationally trying to maximize its well-being, both by moving in the Sugarscape and by exchanging goods with its neighbors. The main differences of this model with a ME market model are not so much at the agent level, but in the way the exchanges take place. First, exchanges are local: agents can only exchange with their neighbors, instead of being able to do it with any agent. And second, the process of determination of the prices and quantities exchanged is a sequential bilateral bargaining process through which each pair of agents agrees on a price and quantity that increases the well-being of both in small steps. This contrasts with the typical ME assumption, as we will see in detail later, of an "invisible hand" that determines a single relative price between sugar and spice, and the optimal quantities to be exchanged for the whole market, that is, for all agents. Or, alternatively, with the assumption that fully rational agents have the capacity to compute the optimal global prices and quantities.

We present here the results of a simulation of the model with movement and trade for fifty periods, with an initial population of 743 agents randomly distributed on a 50 × 50 grid, with metabolic needs of sugar and spice between one and five units, and vision ranges also between one and five. At the beginning of the simulation, between twenty-five and fifty units of sugar and spice are randomly distributed among the agents.

$$p = \sqrt[3]{MRS_A\ MRS_B}$$

The main function of this rule is to moderate the effect of two agents having MRS far away from each other. The quantities exchanged are determined as in Epstein and Axtell (1996), as follows: if $p > 1$ then p units of spice are exchanged for one of sugar; if $p < 1$, then $1/p$ units of sugar are exchanged for one unit of spice.

[8] The process of determination of prices and quantities repeats itself if it improves both agents' welfare and if their MRSs do not crossover or until they equalize.

Figure 2.8 shows the evolution of the population every ten periods during the first fifty periods of the simulation. We can see how the agent population shrinks and clusters around the four peaks of the Sugarscape. This happens through an evolutionary selection process: if we compare the characteristics of the population in the first period against the last, we get that the average vision increases from 2.93 to 2.94, while the average sugar metabolism decreases from 3.03 to 2.32, and that of spice from 3.03 to 2.21. In other words, agents with the highest range of vision and lower metabolic requirements are those that survive. It should also be noted that surviving agents with a higher metabolic need for spice than sugar tend to cluster at peaks where there is more spice than sugar (the northeast and southwest peaks), while agents with more metabolic need for sugar than spice tend to cluster in peaks where there is more sugar (southeast and northwest).

In Table 2.1 we can see the sequence of agreed prices and quantities exchanged between an agent and one of its neighbors during the bilateral process that takes place between them in a simulation period. We see that in this case the bargaining lasted eight rounds, in which the price went from 0.495 to 0.567, while quantities exchanged went from 2.02 kg of sugar per 1 kg of spice to 1.76 kg of sugar per 1 kg of spice. If agents had full rationality, they could agree at once on the price and quantities to exchange, instead of doing it in successive steps. But here we assume that they have bounded rationality, and that therefore they proceed by successive approximations in which small amounts are exchanged in each round of bargaining.

In Figure 2.9 we see the evolution of the average exchange price during fifty simulation periods. Each price condenses information from all prices resulting from exchanges between each agent and its neighbors, and vary from period to period without ever reaching a stable equilibrium.[9] We can also see that the dispersion occurs approximately around a price equal to one.[10]

It should be noted that each of the average prices is far from being a single and stable equilibrium price. Moreover, each is the average of

---

[9] Following Epstein and Axtell (1996), we define as average price the geometric mean of all the prices observed within each period of the simulation. This is done to avoid the influence of outliers (a few prices that occasionally happen to be far away from the mean price).

[10] Since in the simulation there is approximately the same quantity of sugar and spice in the Sugarscape, the symmetry of preferences implicit in the welfare function W, and the symmetry of initial stocks of sugar and spice, imply that the general equilibrium price would be approximately equal to one.

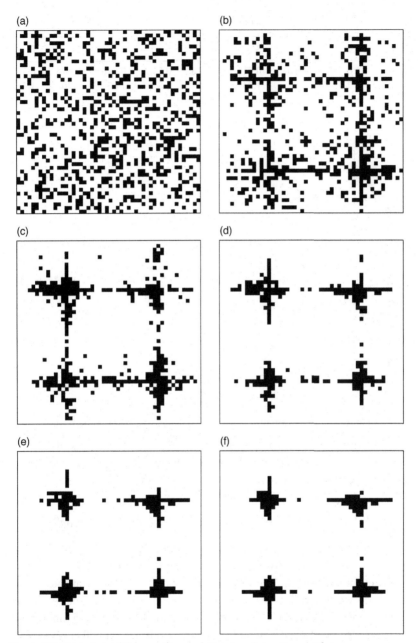

Figure 2.8 Evolution of the agent's population in a Sugarscape with two resources (sugar and spice) and four peaks, with movement and trade rules, over 50 periods (shown the start and end periods, and four intermediate periods)

Table 2.1 *Sequence of bargaining prices between two agents*

Round	1	2	3	4	5	6	7	8
Price	0.495	0.505	0.515	0.526	0.536	0.546	0.556	0.567
Quantity	2.02	2.98	1.94	1.90	1.87	1.85	1.80	1.76

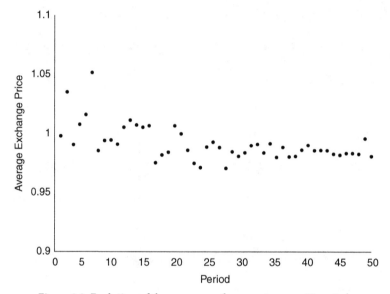

Figure 2.9 Evolution of the average exchange price over 50 periods

many other prices at which each agent exchanged with its neighbors within each period. In other words, within each period and from one period to another, there are multiple prices for the same good.

2.3 A Mainstream Economics Static Exchange Model

Let us now look at a market exchange model like the one presented in the previous section but based on ME assumptions and methods. This will be a static exchange model. As in the previous model, suppose that each agent consumes two different types of goods, sugar and spice, and that each has different preferences for one or the other good, thus valuing them differently. Let's also assume that each agent is a rational optimizer: it will always try to make those exchanges that, given its preferences, give it the highest utility.

Unlike the previous model, let's assume that each agent can exchange goods with any other agent and, moreover, that it can exchange goods in

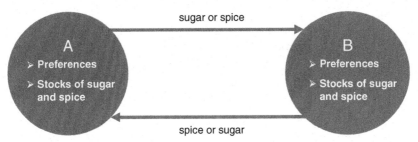

Figure 2.10 An exchange economy with two agents and two goods

different quantities, and simultaneously, with more than one agent. Let's also assume that there is no geography over which the goods are distributed, and on which agents move to collect them. In other words, each agent will no longer be limited to exchanging only with its neighbors, or moving in a restricted environment, because in the absence of a geography the concepts of neighborhood and movement lose meaning.

To start as simply as possible, if we assume that our exchange economy is made up of two agents, A and B, we can represent it with the scheme shown in Figure 2.10. Each agent has preferences for sugar and spice, and has stocks of those goods. According to their preferences and stocks, they will exchange sugar for spice, and vice versa. Of course, the scheme is easily generalizable to any number of agents.

Let's see how to graphically represent and solve this model. Its mathematical representation and solution are in Annex C. Let's begin by representing the sugar market, and start with an agent who wants to buy sugar. For each possible price of sugar, such an agent will be willing to buy some quantity, depending on its preferences and wealth (its wealth is made of the quantities of sugar and spice in its stock). Because it is a rational agent, it will always seek to satisfy its preferences in the best possible way – that is, to maximize its utility – given the budget constraint that is imposed on it by its level of wealth. This rational optimizing behavior will be reflected in the way the agent determines its demand for sugar given its price: at a price it considers high it will demand a small quantity of sugar. At a lower price, it will demand a larger quantity. At an even lower price, it will demand an even higher quantity. And so on.

Both agents A and B, as sugar buyers, will exhibit similar behavior to that just described. Therefore, if we add up their individual demands, we can represent their joint demand (or aggregate demand) for sugar with a downline, as in Figure 2.11. The vertical axis represents the possible prices, while the horizontal axis represents the quantities that would be demanded at each of those prices.

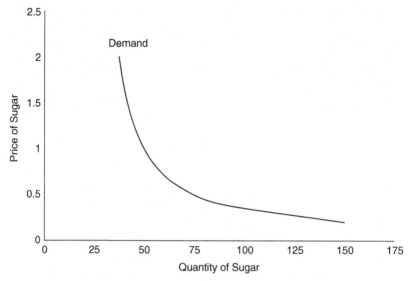

Figure 2.11 The demand for sugar

Let us now think about the supply of sugar in this economy. The aggregate supply of sugar is equal to the sum of the sugar stocks held by agents A and B. Thus, it is a fixed quantity: it will not change whatever the demand, and whatever the price. Therefore, we represent it graphically as a vertical line, meaning that whatever the price of sugar, the available quantity of sugar will be the same. If we assume that the total sugar stock is, for example, equal to 50, then the vertical line will cross the horizontal axis at 50, as shown in Figure 2.12.

Finally, we need an economic institution that makes it possible for those who demand sugar, and those who offer it, to meet. This institution is the market, which we can think of as that place – be physical or virtual – in which agents meet, reveal their demands and supplies, and make exchanges. But a key question arises here: for such exchanges to take place, a price must be set. In the example we are analyzing, we can find that price simply by looking at the sugar market chart, like Figure 2.13, in which we put together the demand and supply curves.

We see that there is only one point on the chart where the lines intersect: where the price is equal to 1 and the quantity exchanged is equal to 50.[11] In other words, there is only one price that makes both demand and supply meet.

[11] As can be seen in Annex C, the price is equal to 1 because we assume that agent's preferences are symmetrical, and that the distribution of sugar and spice stocks is also symmetrical (since we also assume that the stocks of sugar and spice are equal).

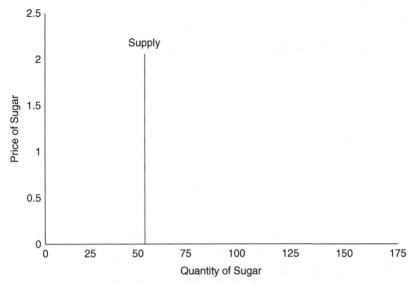

Figure 2.12 The supply of sugar

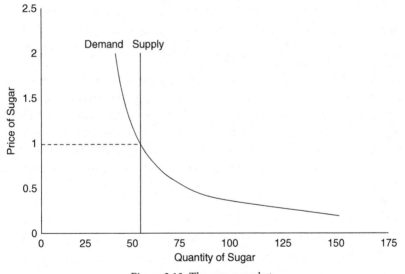

Figure 2.13 The sugar market

That will be the equilibrium price of the sugar market, and the only price at which the buying and selling of sugar will take place. As we can see in Figure 2.14, at a price higher than 1, such as 1.5, there would be fewer agents willing

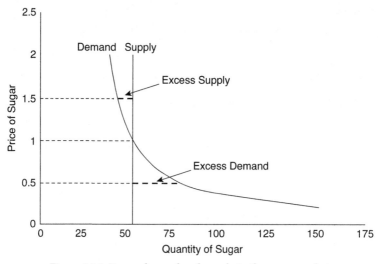

Figure 2.14 Excess demand and supply in the sugar market

to demand sugar, so there would be an excess supply that would be left unsold; whereas, if the price decreased, that excess would disappear. At a price lower than 1, for example 0.5, there would be more agents willing to demand sugar, but that demand would exceed the existing supply, thus there would be an excess demand for sugar; while, if the price were to increase, that excess would disappear. Therefore, there will be no exchanges at any price other than the equilibrium price, at which the demand and supply quantities are equal.

Moreover, in the case represented by the sugar market chart, it would be impossible to think, for example, of a price of 2 and a quantity of 100 units of sugar. That would be a disequilibrium point, and there is no way to achieve it in a typical ME model such as the one presented, which is essentially an equilibrium model. To achieve that point, it would be necessary to shift the aggregate supply and aggregate demand curves. But this would imply that initial resource allocations and/or agent preferences changed, something which is not supposed to happen during the "instant" in which the pricing process takes place.[12]

---

[12] Of course, if we assume some form of external intervention in the market, such as the government imposition of a maximum price for sugar, a disequilibrium situation could arise, since in such a case the price imposed would be below the equilibrium price. Thus, at that price, there would be more demand than supply of sugar (i.e., an excess demand). But both in the AE model that we have seen in the previous section (the Sugarscape model), and in the ME model of market exchange of this section, our goal is to analyze

As we are dealing with a model with two goods, sugar and spice, there will be two markets, each with its corresponding supply and demand curves, and thus their prices and equilibrium quantities. And because agents' preferences and wealth cover both sugar and spice, demands and supplies in such markets will be interconnected: what happens in one market will affect the other. Thus, we are dealing with what is known in ME as a general equilibrium model. A very small one, as it consists of only two goods and therefore two markets. But this example could extend to an economy with many goods, and therefore many interconnected markets, as well as to many agents. In such a case, it will be impossible to solve the model by means of a graphical representation, and it will be necessary to develop and solve its mathematical representation. Anyway, the overall result will be that there will be only one set of equilibrium prices to which all exchanges of goods take place.[13]

We can conclude by highlighting two things, one at the individual level and one at the aggregate level. At the individual level, each agent behaves like a rational and maximizer entity. And at the aggregate level, a global constraint is imposed that aggregate demand and aggregate supply must equalize for trade to take place, so that no surpluses of demand or supply are left. Simply put, individual optimization and global market clearing constraints are the fundamental assumptions of ME when modeling markets.

2.4 A Mainstream Economics Dynamic Model of Production and Consumption

In the previous section, we presented a pure exchange static general equilibrium model, typical of ME. We will now introduce a dynamic model of production and consumption, or a dynamic general equilibrium model, also typical of ME. It will be a relatively simple production and consumption model, with only one good produced and consumed, and two agents: a household and a firm. We assume that these agents are representative agents of all households and of all firms in the economy.

---

and contrast the properties that arise endogenously from them, and not the results from external interventions.

[13] The existence of a single set of equilibrium prices is guaranteed if demand and supply behave normally. In our example, that normality exists because demand is continuous and downward, and supply is continuous and upward, and therefore they cross at a single point. If demand or supply behaved abnormally, for example, if they presented discontinuities, or showed downward and then upward segments, it could be the case that demand and supply do not cross, or do so more than once, resulting in the inexistence of an equilibrium price, or in the existence of multiple equilibrium prices.

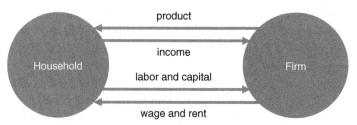

Figure 2.15 A dynamic economy with production and consumption, two representative agents, one good, and two factors of production

That is to say that each represents the aggregation or sum of the behaviors of many households and of many firms. But for such an aggregation to be representative, we have to assume that all households are identical, like all firms, or that they are heterogeneous but behave in such a way that the sum of their decisions is equivalent to the decision of a single household and a single firm. Figure 2.15 gives us a first approximation to the structure of the model. Its mathematical representation and solution are in Annex C.

This is a very simple economy in which one firm produces a single good, which is consumed by the household. The household is a supplier of labor and the owner of capital (machinery, tools, facilities, etc.). The firm hires labor and rents capital from the household, and pays wage and rent to it. Household income is then equal to the sum of wage and rent. With this income, the household buys the good produced by the firm and consumes it. The firm's profit is equal to the difference between its income from selling the good and its cost from paying wage and rent.[14]

The household has an important decision at its disposal in each period: it may decide to spend all its income on consumption, or to save a part of it. This would allow the household to lend its saving to the firm. The firm will transform it into investment, that is, in an increase in the stock of capital. And the increased capital stock will allow the firm to increase the quantity of the good produced in the next period, and thus pay to the household an extra rent for its saving. Finally, in the next period, the household will have an increased income, and therefore will be able to consume more of the good. Figure 2.16 shows a schematic representation of this dynamic process.

---

[14] We assume that the firm operates in perfect competition, so that its profit, if it behaves optimally, is equal to zero. This may seem paradoxical, but we must bear in mind that we are assuming that the firm is owned by the household that rents the capital stock to the firm.

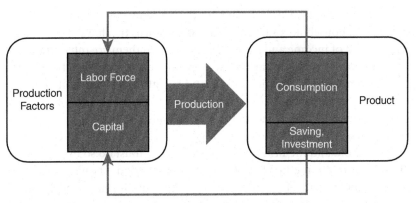

Figure 2.16 Outline of the growth dynamic of an economy with two factors of production and a product for consumption or savings/investment

In this scheme of economic dynamic, we see that the production process employs the factors of production (labor and capital) to generate product (in this economy, the product is composed by one good only). One part of the product is used to satisfy the consumption of the labor force, and the other part that is not consumed – that is, it is saved – is invested to increase the capital stock of the economy. So, from one period to the next, the economy grows.

What are the goals of the behavior of the household and the firm, which make this economic dynamic possible? The goal of the household is to maximize its well-being, which in this model is equivalent to consuming as much product as possible in all future periods of its life – which we will assume is infinite – but always considering that lower consumption today implies more future consumption, and vice versa. So, if we assume that C represents consumption over a period, the household seeks to maximize the series:[15]

$$C_1 + C_2 + C_3 + C_4 + ... + C_{infinity}$$

The goal of the firm is to maximize its profits throughout its life, which we also assume is infinite. So, if we assume that π represents each period profit, the firm tries to maximize the series:

$$\pi_1 + \pi_2 + \pi_3 + \pi_4 + ... + \pi_{infinity}$$

---

[15] Usually, as can be seen in Annex C, a time discount rate is applied in each period, to account for the relative value of present consumption with respect to future consumption.

Given the structure and dynamic of the economy we are analyzing, we can see that household and firm decisions, as well as the flows of goods and services and of income and expenditures between them are intertwined, in a similar way to what we saw in the previous section in the static general equilibrium model, in which prices and quantities in different markets were connected. But here the entanglement is more complex, since it is synchronous and diachronic: there must be consistency between decisions within each period, but also between all periods. That is to say that when the household and the firm make decisions, they must do so by looking at the whole present picture, but also at all future periods simultaneously.

In a similar fashion to the static general equilibrium model of the previous section, this dynamic model also imposes global constraints: aggregate supply and demand must always be equal and markets must clear. In other words, it is assumed that all labor and capital supplied by the household in each period is employed by the firm, the whole quantity of the good produced and offered by the firm in each period is bought by the household, and all savings is transformed into investment. Thus, the prices that solve the model should be exactly those that ensure that these constraints are met.

However, unlike the static general equilibrium model, in which the solution was a single-point equilibrium of supply and demand, in this model the solution is a set of dynamic equilibrium trajectories of prices and quantities. For example, Figure 2.17 shows the dynamic model solution for a set of initial conditions and given parametric values, and for twenty-five periods. Details on this solution are in Annex C.

We can see the trajectories of quantities (the capital stock, consumption, and product) and the price trajectories (the wage and the interest rate). Numbers on the vertical axis can be interpreted as quantities expressed in units of the good produced by the economy, except for the interest rate that is a percentage (e.g., a value equal to 0.03 means 3 percent per period).

For each period there is a single set of prices and quantities. And for each variable, there is a well-defined temporal path. From the zero period, the interest rate follows a downward transitional trajectory to stabilize at a constant level. While the other variables follow an upward trajectory in which they all grow at a same steady rate. In other words, the proportions between them remain constant over time and forever.

All trajectories are equilibrium paths, both in their transitional stage and when they stabilize at a constant value or when they grow at a constant rate. And there's no way to deviate from them. The latter can be seen in an

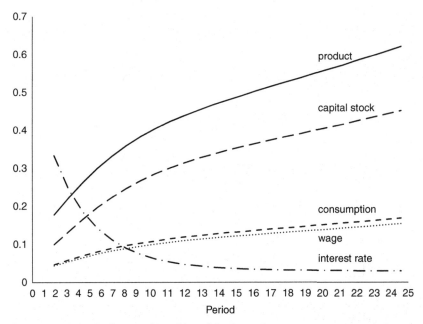

Figure 2.17 Evolution of variables of the dynamic economy over 25 periods

alternative representation of the dynamics of the model, which is called a phase diagram, a widely used graphical instrument for visualizing the qualitative properties of dynamic models.

In Figure 2.18, we see the phase diagram for two of the model variables: the capital stock and consumption. The horizontal axis corresponds to the capital stock (K), and the vertical axis to the consumption level (C). We can think of this diagram as a representation of alternative paths of the joint dynamics of the two variables. Each point on the diagram surface represents a state of the model (in this case, the joint state of the capital stock and consumption), and the arrows show the direction of motion to another state. There are infinite lines that cross the diagram in different directions. In the figure, we show only a few. A more developed diagram is in Annex C.

Assume that in the initial period (period 0) the economy starts from a capital stock equal to K_0. In that same period, the household must decide how much to consume. We see that there are three possible options on the chart: it can choose C0x, C0SP, or C0z. If it chooses C0x, the capital stock and consumption will move together along the path marked by the X-curve. But that implies that after some time, consumption will be zero, so that the household would perish. If it chooses C0z, the joint movement

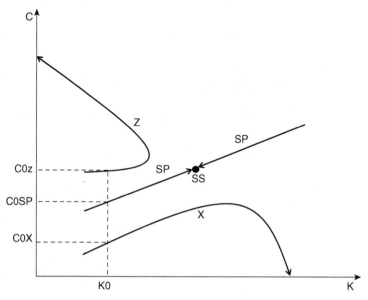

Figure 2.18 Simplified phase diagram of the evolution of consumption and the capital stock in the dynamic economy

will be along the Z-curve, so that after some time the capital stock would disappear, and the economy could not continue producing. Now let's look carefully at the SP path, which is the called saddle path. We see that it has two directions of movement toward the SS point: one coming from above and one coming from below. The SS point represents the steady state of the economy. From the moment that point is reached, all variables remain unchanged (as was the case with the interest rate on the trajectory chart we saw previously), or they will grow in a balanced way (as was the case with the other variables in the same chart). Therefore, if the household chooses the consumption level C0SP, the economy will move over its optimal dynamic path until it reaches the steady state of growth. Thus, if the household behaves as an optimizer trying to maximize its well-being in the present and in every possible future, and if it has an unlimited capacity for acquiring and processing information to determine, from the infinite possible paths, the only one that would put the economy on an optimal equilibrium dynamic, then it will choose, in the initial period, a consumption level exactly equal to C0SP.

It is obvious that when the model's variables are in the steady state, the economy is in equilibrium (or, dynamically, on a balanced growth path).

But it is worth mentioning that even when the economy is on the saddle path, which is a transitional path toward the steady state, it is also in equilibrium, since even on the saddle path all markets clear: there are no excess demands or supplies. It is then a transitional path in which each good or factor of production has, in each period, an equilibrium price.

2.5 Contrasts

In the last two sections we have seen two typical ME general equilibrium models: one static and one dynamic. In both models we saw that all prices and quantities (the ones of sugar and spice in the static model, and the trajectories of wages, the interest rate, production, consumption, investment, and the capital stock in the dynamic model) are equilibrium prices and quantities. However, how does the process through which all agents trading goods and services in those models come to do so at equilibrium prices, and not at any other prices? What information-gathering and processing capabilities are required for agents to achieve such a result?

There are two ways to address this issue. In one, which we will call the central auctioneer metaphor, not much sophistication is required by each agent; in the other, which we will call the agent with full rationality model, large quantities of information and huge computational capabilities are required.

Let's start with the central auctioneer metaphor. It is assumed that each agent informs, to a mechanism called the central auctioneer, how much of each good it would be willing to sell or buy at every possible price. With this information, the auctioneer computes the prices and equilibrium quantities of each good and communicates them to all the agents, who carry out the exchanges at those prices and in those quantities. Thus, the central auctioneer metaphor would be a more formal equivalent of Adam Smith's invisible hand metaphor, that hand that leads the market toward the best allocation of economic resources in a society.

This way of looking at the process of price and quantity determination leads to the idea that each agent has little information and limited computational capacity: it only sees the prices that are given to it by the central auctioneer, and only decides, taking into account those prices and its individual demand or supply functions, the quantities that it will demand or supply, the ones which will consume or invest, etc.

But no market has a centralized coordination device like the central auctioneer. On the contrary, the market is supposed to be a totally decentralized mechanism of exchange and pricing. Therefore, if we dispense with the metaphor of the central auctioneer, this would lead us to make a completely different characterization of agents. Indeed, in the absence of a central coordination mechanism, we should assume that each agent has full information about the market and an unlimited computation capacity; that is to say, it is capable of access to all the individual supply and demand functions from the other agents and can itself compute the equilibrium prices and quantities, and finally, based on those prices, decide how much to buy or sell of each good. In this way, each agent becomes an agent with full rationality, in a way equivalent to a central auctioneer.

There is also another issue worth noting. In the general equilibrium models of ME, all agents interact globally: every agent can exchange goods with all agents and not only with a small group, as was the case in AE models. However, such interaction is somehow virtual: all existing information about supplies and demands is processed by the central auctioneer, or by each fully rational agent, to compute the equilibrium prices, but it is only once those prices are determined that the exchanges of goods (purchases and sales) or other economic decisions (such as production, consumption, and investment) take place. In other words, in ME models there are no transitional dynamics in which exchanges take place at disequilibrium prices. Indeed, as we saw earlier, in the static ME model it was impossible to think of an out-of-equilibrium price, and in the dynamic model phase diagram it was impossible to be out of the steady state or out of the saddle path. On the contrary, in the Sugarscape, a typical model of AE, we observed local interactions between agents and a multitude of effective (i.e., non-virtual) exchange prices outside of what would have been the overall equilibrium price of the model.

From what we have seen so far, we can conclude that there is an interesting first contrast between the AE and the ME about the rationality of the agents and their forms of coordination. In the Sugarscape model, agents have bounded rationality: they only capture and process information from a small environment, and solve very simple problems, such as searching their neighborhood for the free cell with more resources available, adding to their stock the quantities of sugar or spice found, and subtracting the quantities consumed; or more complex problems, such as exchanging resources with their neighbors trying to optimize their behavior constrained by their available resources. But under no circumstances is there a centralized coordination mechanism. On the contrary, the general equilibrium models we analyzed, typical of ME, require either the assumption of the existence of a central auctioneer with a huge capacity for acquiring and processing information, or that each agent has such capacity, that is, that each is an agent with full rationality. A second contrast has to do with the fact that in the AE model seen before there is a transitional disequilibrium dynamic, while in the ME models, disequilibrium is not possible. Finally, a third contrast is that in the AE model there is an evolutionary process: only those agents with greater vision range and lower metabolic requirements survive, while in the ME models we presented the evolutionary process is absent.

3

Artificial Games

In the previous chapter, we presented an AE model in which artificial agents interacted through markets, and then contrasted it with similar ME models. In this chapter, we present models in which agents interact through games, but proceed in reverse. We will first introduce a typical ME model known as the prisoner's dilemma, in which agents interact through a classic game, and then contrast it with an artificial evolutionary game based on the same dilemma.

3.1 A Classic Game

Next, we present a simple example of a classic game named the prisoner's dilemma, with only two agents, who we call players. Suppose the two players are criminals who have committed a crime and fallen into the hands of the police, and that they are about to be questioned separately from each other. Both offenders previously agreed that, if caught, neither would confess to their crime or blame the other. Each prisoner will have at her disposal a strategy with two possible actions: cooperate with her accomplice, honoring their agreement and denying any involvement in the crime by either, or defect from the agreement, denying her involvement in the crime, but blaming the accomplice.

Figure 3.1 shows a representation of the game in the form a payoff matrix. For each player there is a strategy with two possible actions: defect (D) or cooperate (C). Each action has an associated number that represents its payoff. We assume that the maximum time to which a prisoner can be sentenced is five years, and the payoffs represent the reduction in time corresponding to each action. The darker cells represent the strategies and payoffs of player 1, the lighter ones of player 2.

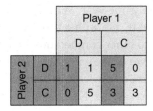

Figure 3.1 Payoff matrix of the evolutionary prisoner's dilemma game with two players

According to what we see in Figure 3.1, if player 1 applies action C (cooperates with her accomplice denying any involvement of both in the crime), and Player 2 does the same, each will get a three-year reduction in the corresponding prison sentence, as the police believe they were both involved in the crime, but need their confession for justice to apply the full sentence.

If player 1 applies action D (defects from the previous agreement, and blames everything on her accomplice) and player 2 does the same, both get a sentence reduction of only one year, as this confirms that both are guilty, but the sentence is reduced a little because justice does not have the confession of any.

If player 1 cooperates (does not confess to the crime) but player 2 defects (she says she is innocent and blames everything on her accomplice), then player 1 gets no time reduction while player 2 gets a reduction of five years and goes free. The opposite happens if player 2 cooperates and player 1 defects.

The optimal solution of this game is obtained assuming that each player chooses her best action, that is the action that gives her the greatest payoff, given the action chosen by her opponent. Let's start with player 1 and ask ourselves what her best action is. Let's assume that player 1 applies action D. If player 2 applies action D, player 1 gets a reduction of one year, while if player 2 applies action C, she gets a five-year reduction. On the other hand, if player 1 applies action C, she will get no reduction of years if player 2 applies action D and one of three years if player 2 applies action C. Thus, the best action to apply for player 1 is D, since given her possible actions, and given the possible actions of player 2, it is the one that gives her the greatest payoff, that is, the greatest reduction in time, equal to five years.

If we repeat this exercise, but now from the point of view of player 2, we will get the same result. In other words, her best action will be to defect. But then, and paradoxically, by virtue of the payoff structure of our example, the solution of the game is (D,D), that is when both players defect, which gives both a payoff of only one year. Whereas if they had cooperated the solution would have been (C,C), with a three-year payoff for both.

Compared to (D,D), no other combination of actions would be rational and stable, as the incentives of the game are such that it is always, from an individual and selfish point of view, more beneficial to defect. This is what is known in game theory as the Nash equilibrium – that solution (or solutions, since in some cases there may be more than one) in which expectations and actions of all players are mutually compatible, and that offers no one an incentive to change her action.

There are numerous applications of the prisoner's dilemma game in economics. For example, we can think of the situation of two oligopolistic firms that have a price agreement: they compromise to cooperate by maintaining a high price for their product and sharing market demand in equal parts. But because a reduction in the price by one company would imply that it would get more demand for its product and therefore a greater total profit, it will have an incentive to defect from its agreement and thus take consumers away from the other firm. But the same will happen with the other firm. So, both will reduce their price, each staying, as before, with half the market, but now making lower profits. There are also applications of this type of game in sociology and political science.

We exemplified with a simple game involving only two players, each with a strategy of only two actions. But the game can be generalized to multiple agents with multiple actions. In such a case the solution would be more demanding and require a mathematical representation, specifying the optimal reaction functions of each player against the possible strategies of all other players, then finding the Nash equilibrium.

3.2 An Artificial Evolutionary Game

Let us now maintain the structural characteristics of our game, but introduce some modifications to transform it into an artificial evolutionary game, following a tradition initiated in the social sciences by Robert Axelrod (1997). Unlike the previous section, where the game was played only once by players with full rationality, we will now introduce an evolutionary prisoner's dilemma game that is played many times by successive generations of players absolutely dumb or hardheads without any strategic view of the game. Each of these players will play without knowing, or paying attention to, the game's payoffs or the actions and strategies of her opponents. In other words, she will decide her actions regardless of what the other players do. For example, suppose we have two players, who will play the same game ten times in a row. And that the first player follows this strategy:

CCCCCCCCCC

that is, in each of the ten times, plays the same action: cooperate, while the second player follows this strategy:

CCCCDDCDCD

which implies that the first four times her action is to cooperate, the next two times defect, then her actions alternate.

Now let's change the way agents' actions are represented. Instead of letters, let's use binary numbers (i.e., only zeros and ones), so that we can apply a method known as genetic algorithm. We proceed as follows: a number one instead of C, and a zero instead of D. Thus, the representation of the above strategies is, for the first player:

1111111111

and, for the second player:

1111001010

Let's name the sequence of actions as the chromosome of each player. Each player is then represented with a ten-bit-long chromosome, where each gene represents an action (one if cooperates, zero if defects). In this way we can interpret the chromosome of each player as her game strategy (i.e., a sequence of actions).

Suppose each generation is made up of twenty players. Within each generation, each player will play ten times against each member of her generation, following the strategy implicit in her chromosome. Thus, player 1 will play the same game ten times against player 2, then against player 3, etc., until she finishes playing against player 20. And so, will the other players. Payoffs earned in each game will accumulate for each player. For example, suppose that player 1 starts playing against player 2, and that each has the following chromosomes, which as we know represent their game strategy:

Player 1: 1111111111
Player 2: 1010101010

In the first game, the action (or gene) of player 1 is represented by a number one (cooperate), and player's 2 action also by a number one. Given the values of the payoff matrix for the prisoner's dilemma game presented in Figure 3.1, this implies that each player, playing the cooperate action, will get a payoff equal to three. In the second game, the action of player 1 is also to cooperate, but that of player 2 is represented by a zero, that is, her action is to defect. Thus, according to the values in that matrix, the payoff for player 1 will be zero, while for player 2 will be five.

Thus far, the accumulated payoff of player 1 is equal to 3 + 0 = 3, while the payoff of player 2 is 3 + 5 = 8. In the third game, player 1 cooperates again (as her gene is equal to one), but player 2 changes her action from defecting to cooperating (because her gene is now zero). Thus, the payoff for each is equal to three. This results in player 1's accumulated payoff being 3 + 0 + 3 = 6, while for player 2 is 3 + 5 + 3 = 11. If we continue until we complete all ten games between these two players, we will have that the accumulated payoff of player 1 will be equal to 15, and the accumulated payoff of player 2 will be equal to 40. As we said before, this procedure will be repeated for each player within each generation.

Once the round of games is over for each generation, the two players who have accumulated the highest payoffs are selected. This pair of players will be the parents of the next generation. This generation will also consist of twenty players (i.e., the parents will have twenty children). The chromosomes (strategies) of the children will be the result of the crossover of the chromosomes of their parents. For example, if parents have the following chromosomes:

Father: 1111100000
Mother: 0000011111

and if we define genetic inheritance in such a way that children inherit the first half of the father's chromosomes and the second half of the mother's chromosomes, the children's base chromosome will be:

Child: 1111111111

In turn, we could introduce random mutations that affect some of the children's chromosomes, so that each child will have the same chromosomal base, but she will have some difference with her siblings. For example, if the mutation affects only the last gene, which in the case of this child would switch from zero to one, then we will have:

Mutated child: 1111111110

The new generation thus created will replay as described and the process will be repeated for a given number of generations. What we have just described succinctly is a simple example of what is known as genetic algorithm. In Chapter 6 we will present this type of algorithm in more detail.

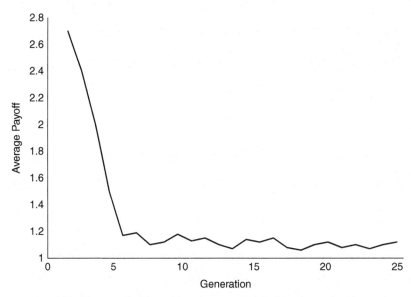

Figure 3.2 Average payoff of the evolutionary prisoner's dilemma game over 25 generations

Let's see what happens if we perform a simulation that starts with a generation of twenty players, with a random distribution of chromosomes, and which lasts for twenty-five generations.[1] Figure 3.2 shows the average payoff earned in each generation. On the vertical axis we see the value of the average payoff, and horizontally the corresponding generation number. We can see that the average payoff in the first generation is approximately equal to 2.7, but that as games are played and generations evolve, it declines rapidly. From generation five, we see that it continues to fluctuate randomly around a value very close to one. And this is the value, as we saw in the previous section of this chapter, corresponding to the Nash equilibrium!

Figure 3.3 shows, for each generation, the chromosome of the player with the highest accumulated payoffs in each generation, that is, the most adapted or evolved player. More precisely, what we see on the vertical axis is the decimal representation of that player's chromosome. By decimal representation we mean that we make the binary number of ten bits of length composed of zeros and ones representing the chromosome of a player equivalent within

[1] For a computational implementation in MATLAB of this evolutionary game, see Kendrick, Mercado, and Amman (2006), pp. 201–222.

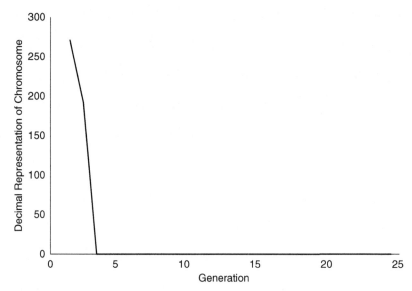

Figure 3.3 Evolution of the decimal representation of the chromosome of the player with the highest accumulated payoff in each generation, over 25 generations

the decimal system. For example, the binary number of ten bits all equal to zero (corresponding to an always defecting player) is represented by the decimal number zero. While the binary number of ten bits all equal to one (corresponding to an always cooperating player) is represented by the decimal number 1023. All other possible values of the player's chromosomes shall be between this maximum value and the minimum value equal to zero.[2]

We can see that the simulation started with a value close to 270, much larger than zero but quite lower that 1023, indicating that the initial generation contained a mixture of cooperators and defectors. However, we see that these values fall quickly, and approximately from generation three are equal to zero. This means that from there, game after game and generation after generation, only those players whose chromosomes are made of genes all equal to zero survive. That is, players whose strategy is

---

[2] To transform a binary number into its decimal representation, each position of the binary number is multiplied, from left to right, by the corresponding ascending power of the number two. For example, for the binary number 1011, we proceed as follows:

$$1 \times 2^3 + 0 \times 2^2 + 1 \times 2^1 + 1 \times 2^0 = 1 \times 8 + 0 \times 4 + 1 \times 2 + 1 \times 1 = 8 + 0 + 2 + 1 = 11$$

so that we get a decimal representation equal to the number 11.

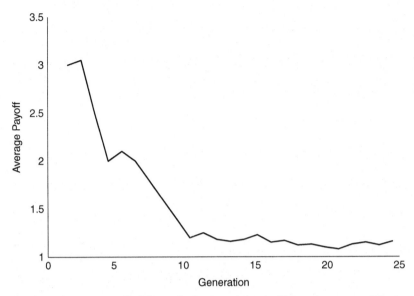

Figure 3.4 Average payoff of the evolutionary prisoner's dilemma game over 25 generations with an initial population in which all players are cooperators

always to defect. And this strategy is precisely the one corresponding to the Nash equilibrium!

We could think that the observed results are due to the start of the simulation with a random number of cooperators that was not enough to generate a dynamic of sustained cooperation over time, and that if we changed that initial configuration the result would be substantially altered and we would not reach the Nash equilibrium.

To test this hypothesis, we performed another simulation in which all the players of the initial population are cooperators. As in the previous simulation, children's chromosomes result from the combination of their parents' chromosomes, and random mutations occur in some of the children's genes. The following two figures show the results. We can see in Figure 3.4 that, as in the previous simulation, the average payoff converges toward a value close to one.

And we also see in Figure 3.5 that the decimal representation of the chromosome begins at a very high value – equal to 1023 – which as we saw previously corresponds to the chromosome of a purely cooperating player. We also see that, although more slowly than in the previous simulation, the genetic makeup of the population converges toward one in which they are

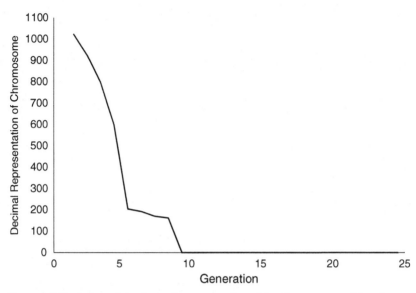

Figure 3.5 Evolution of the decimal representation of the chromosome of the player with the highest accumulated payoffs in each generation, over 25 generations, with an initial population in which all players are cooperators

all defectors. Thus, no matter what the initial genetic configuration of the population is, the result is always the same.

Remarkably, we can conclude that the population of this artificial evolutionary game with players with bounded rationality (actually, with extremely limited cognitive ability) and who interact locally over time (i.e., only within a generation) converges toward the Nash equilibrium. That is, convergence occurs at the same equilibrium that we obtained earlier in a game with players with full rationality and global interactions, in which the optimal strategy was to defect and the payoff equal to one, but now it occurs in an evolutionary dynamic process of "natural selection" and through disequilibrium situations, in the sense that in some periods the results of the game are different from the Nash equilibrium.[3]

---

[3] Another interesting case – although without an evolutionary process – in which simple minded artificial agents reach the same equilibrium situation as agents with full rationality is the one pioneered by Dhananjay Gode and Shyam Sunder (Gode and Sunder, 1993). In this case, artificial agents with "zero intelligence" participate in double auction market experiments (a typical example of a double auction market is the stock market). Agents submit random bids and offers to a market institution, and imposing a budget constraint (i.e., not permitting agents to sell below their costs or buy above their values) is sufficient to

3.3 Contrasts

It's important to review now some features of the games we have just analyzed. In the first game, typical of classical game theory and therefore of ME, we find something like what we saw in the market economy models presented in Chapter 2, also typical of ME. Each agent – each player – is supposed to know everything about the game: it is informed of all the strategies and payoffs of the other agents, it knows that they are all selfish, and it also knows that all other agents have the same information as it has. And taking all this into account, chooses its optimal behavior, conditional to all possible actions of the other agents. Therefore, we can say that, for each agent its vision range is global (it has perfect and complete information about the whole game), its interactions are also global (it plays with all other players simultaneously), and it is fully rational (it can process all existing information in order to determine its optimal action). This contrasts with the artificial evolutionary game we presented earlier. In this game, the vision range and interactions between agents and their rationality are bounded: each agent interacts sequentially with the others and carries out its strategy without paying any attention to the characteristics of the game or to the strategies of its opponents. Finally, in the classic game, which is an eminently static game, we reach the Nash equilibrium instantly, without going through any disequilibrium situation, while in the artificial evolutionary game such an equilibrium is achieved, but after a transitional evolutionary disequilibrium dynamic.[4]

raise the allocative efficiency of the auctions close to 100 percent, and to achieve the same standard equilibrium prices as predicted by ME theory. This result shows that many market features may rely as much, or even more, on institutional design than on agents' fully rational behavior.

[4] Artificial evolutionary games like the one we presented in this chapter are games in which the evolution of a population of players (and/or their strategies) with bounded rationality, is computationally simulated, and often give rise to transitional disequilibrium dynamics or, as we will see in Chapter 7, to complex dynamics. Artificial evolutionary games differ in methods from evolutionary game theory, which is a theory pioneered in the field of biology by Ronald Fisher, Richard Lewontin, and, in its contemporary form, by John Maynard Smith (1982), and later applied in economics and in the social sciences. This theory focuses on the mathematical modeling of evolutionary processes using as its main tool of analysis the concept of evolutionary stable strategy (a strategy that once adopted by all individuals in a population cannot be substituted or invaded by a different strategy). Evolutionary game theory differs in turn from classical game theory (which is a fundamental part of the theoretical core of ME, as we expose in Annex B, and of which we saw an example in Section 3.1), in that the latter one focuses on the mathematical modeling of strategically interacting agents with full rationality. For an introductory textbook to classical and evolutionary game theory, see Gintis (2009).

4

Artificial Economics versus Mathematics?

In the Introduction to this book, as well as in the previous chapters, we contrasted the assumptions, models, and dynamics on which AE and ME tend to focus. We opposed the assumptions of full rationality, global interactions, and equilibrium dynamics of ME, against those of bounded rationality, local interactions, and disequilibrium dynamics of AE. In this chapter, we want to focus on the methodological and instrumental contrasts between AE and ME.[1]

4.1 Methods and Instruments: Artificial Economics versus Mainstream Economics

The modeling style of ME makes heavy use of the imposition of global constraints, which usually take the form of mathematical equations, to capture the behavior of the economic system being analyzed, for example, by establishing that aggregate supply and demand must equalize in each market. This approach is useful when the system being modeled converges over time toward states that are invariant (i.e., they repeat themselves, such as, for example, a stable market equilibrium) so they can often be described as if they experience global constraints on behavior.

In contrast, AE's methodology is based on specifying agents' behaviors through rules and local interactions between them. From these rules and interactions, aggregate evolutionary phenomena are generated that may or may not converge to an equilibrium, so no global restrictions can be imposed on them a priori.[2]

---

[1] For systematic presentations and discussions of the methodology of ME, see Blaug (1992) and Hausman (1992).

[2] In Wolfram (2002), pp. 210 and 342, there is a discussion of the difference between constraint-based systems and systems based on behavioral rules.

ME methodology is sometimes considered as top-down, because of the imposition of global constraints and, in its typical general equilibrium models, because of the assumption of existence of a central auctioneer from which agents take prices. In contrast, AE methodology is viewed as bottom-up, due to the non-imposition of global constraints and the generation of prices from local interactions. But these spatial metaphors (top-down, bottom-up) are quite generic and not very rigorous.

It is also often stated that the methodology and instruments of ME are essentially mathematical, in contrast to those of AE, which are fundamentally computational.

In ME, an agent is an entity specialized in optimization, who tries to maximize its utility subject to a budget constraint. An economic model is a model of interaction between agents – for example, a set of interconnected markets – which is usually specified as a system of equations; an economic equilibrium, that is, a feasible state of the economic model, is a solution to such a system of equations. Therefore, mathematical techniques of static and dynamic optimization, and static and dynamic equation systems, are fundamental instruments for ME. In other words, the way ME thinks of agents and their interactions has a lot to do with the possibility of modeling them with instruments from classical mathematics.

This contrasts with the methodology and instruments of AE. In AE an agent is a computational object defined by an information set and processing rules, which may or may not be oriented to the optimization of its behavior. Agents, as well as their forms of interaction and their spatial and temporal environments, are programmed and simulated computationally, so that the economic system evolves from one period to another, and from one state to another, as a result of the sequential application of its more basic behavioral rules. Thus, the fundamental instruments of AE are algorithms, software, and computational hardware. In other words, AE's methods and instruments come primarily from computer science, although it should be noted that, as we will see, there is a strong link between computer science and mathematics.

4.2 Computers versus Mathematics?

To get into such a link, a good starting point is to ask questions about what an AE model is, what a computer program is, and ultimately, from a general point of view, what a computer is. An AE model is in fact an algorithm, encoded in a program written in a programming language, which runs on a computer. Let's analyze each of the concepts that make up this phrase.

An algorithm is an ordered and finite list of operations that allows us to find the solution to a problem. Its constituent elements are an initial state, successive and well-defined steps, and a final state that is the solution of the problem. A program is a set of instructions for a computer that implements an algorithm. And a programming language is a set of symbols, syntactic rules (which define the structure of supported combinations of symbols), and semantic rules (which define the meaning of elements and expressions) used to control the behavior of a computer. But what is that device we call a computer, capable of simulating an AE model by running an algorithm, encoded in a program written in a programming language? It can be an electronic machine, a mechanical device, or a person. For example, if we want to compute the multiplication of two numbers, it is enough to have the appropriate algorithm (in this case a procedure that uses the rules of multiplication) executed by a person who uses pencil and paper, a mechanical calculator, or a digital computer. However, the fact that an algorithm can be implemented in such diverse ways gives us an indication that what is relevant is not the medium itself, but that there may be something in common to all of them, more general in nature, associated with the fact of computing.

It was Alan Turing who captured this idea (even before the existence of what we now know as computers) in a famous 1937 article (Turing, 1937), and developed a mathematical model of a universal computing device named the Turing machine. This "machine" is a very simple formal model, but it represents what any computer, even the most advanced contemporary computers, can do. Its elements are a tape of infinite length, made of cells containing symbols (typically zeros and ones, or a blank space); a head that can read and write symbols on the tape and move it left and right; a record that stores the state the Turing machine is in; and a very simple instruction table, named a transition function, which contains the instructions of deleting or writing a symbol, moving the tape left or right, and changing the state or staying in it.

Table 4.1 shows us a very simple transition function for a Turing machine that, given a sequence of zeros and ones, it just reverses its order. The machine has only three symbols (0, 1, and B, which indicates a blank space) and three states (0, 1, and End). From the first row of the table, we can infer that, if the machine is in state 0 and reads the symbol B, it must write the B symbol instead (i.e., leave it as it is) move the tape to the left (L), and transition to state 1. From the second row we have that, if the machine is in state 0 and reads the 0 symbol, it must write the symbol 1 instead, move the tape to the right (R), and stay in the 0 state. Etc.

Table 4.1 *Transition function of a Turing machine that, given a sequence of zeros and ones, reverses its order*

State	Symbol	Writes	Move Tape Toward	Next State
0	B	B	L	1
0	0	1	R	0
0	1	0	R	0
1	B	B	R	End
1	0	1	L	1
1	1	0	L	1

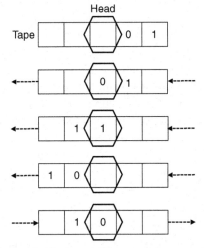

Figure 4.1 Head and tape of a Turing machine operating according to the transition function in Table 4.1, that reverses the order of a sequence of two numbers in four movements

Remember that the Turing machine operates on a tape of infinite length, and suppose that Figure 4.1 show successive images of only five elements of it. The hexagon with thick edges represents the machine head. Suppose that there are written two symbols to the right of the head (0 and 1), that the machine is in the initial state 0, and reading the symbol B (a blank space). The arrows indicate where the tape is moving, and the successive tape images show us the result of applying, step by step and from the given initial conditions, the instructions in the table. As we see, the result is the reversal of the initial sequence of numbers, which goes from (0,1) to (1,0).

We should note that while the words *tape* and *head* would seem to refer to a physical device, we are dealing with a formal system, a mathematical model, whose concrete implementation can be made through various devices.[3] The remarkable thing about a Turing machine is that, despite its simplicity, it is capable of performing any computing procedure, however complex. We only need to expand the transition table. This can be at first glance disconcerting, if we consider that a digital computer can be programmed to solve difficult calculations, simulate extremely complex models, display graphics and animations, and do many other things. However, we should be aware that computer programs written in languages such as JAVA or C[++] are converted before or during execution in low-level programs written in binary code. And that, ultimately, that code materializes in electronic circuits consisting of many gates that can be in two states: open or closed. Roughly speaking, what happens in the hardware of a modern digital computer, when running a program, is a myriad of binary operations (open/close) and thus extremely simple.

Remember that we previously defined an algorithm as an ordered and finite list of operations that allow us to find the solution to a problem. More formally, an algorithm can also be defined as a procedure for calculating a mathematical function. Indeed, it is a procedure that transforms input data into output data, where the former constitutes the problem and the latter the solution. Input and output data can be represented by symbols. Particularly interesting is the symbolic representation by sequences of natural numbers. In this way, an algorithm can be conceptualized as a defined mathematical function on the set of natural numbers, or on a subset of this. That is, seen in this way, a natural number encodes either a problem or its solution, and an algorithm is a procedure for calculating the function that transforms a problem (an input number) into a solution (an output number).

For example, suppose we have an algorithm that transforms an adjective into its opposite (good to bad, passive into aggressive, cute to ugly), and we have a database consisting of six elements in an ordered table as shown in Table 4.2.

Given an adjective as input, for example, "passive," our algorithm will search the left column of the table for the matching word, then it will look

---

[3] In mathematical notation, a Turing machine is a four-tuple $(Q, T, q0, \delta)$ where Q is a finite set of states; T is a finite set of symbols; $q0$ is the initial state; and δ is a transition function that maps $Q \times T$ to $[Q \times T \times \{L, R\}]$. Depending on the present state and the present symbol to which the head is pointing, the Turing machine will move to a new state, change (or leave unaltered) the symbol on the tape, and then move the head left (L) or right (R).

Table 4.2 *A simple ordered database*

good	bad
passive	aggressive
cute	ugly

Table 4.3 *A simple ordered and numbered database*

1	good	4	bad
2	passive	5	aggressive
3	cute	6	ugly

for the corresponding word in the same row, but in the right column, and return as output the adjective "aggressive." Now suppose that we numerically code our database as in Table 4.3, associating a number to each adjective.

Let us now define a very simple mathematical function that for each number it receives as input returns a number that is equal to the number received plus three. In mathematical notation, where x is the input number (which can take values between one and three), and where f means "function of," our function can be written as:

$$f(x) = x + 3$$

So, if the function receives the number one, it returns the number four. If it gets the number two, it returns the number five. That, by the equivalences defined in Table 4.3, is equivalent to receiving the adjective "passive" and returning the adjective "aggressive."

It should be noted that usually the algorithms that a computer runs are recursive. Recursion is a central idea in computer science. It refers to an algorithm or program that during its run calls itself repeatedly, so that the problem to be solved is addressed by a succession of runs, but of decreasing size and therefore simpler. Thus, the complexity of the original problem to be solved is significantly reduced.

For example, suppose we want to compute the factorial of a number, which is the product of all the natural numbers less than itself, until we reach the number 1. The factorial of number 4 is equal to $4 \times 3 \times 2 \times 1$, so it is equal to the number 24. The factorial of an n number can be obtained using a recursive algorithm (or, equivalently, a recursive computer program) such as the following:

```
Program factorial(n);
    If n is greater than one,
    returns the result of n x factorial(n-1),
    otherwise returns 1;
End of program;
```

We see that within the program named *factorial*(n) a call to the same program is made, for a value less than n in one unit, by *factorial*(n–1). The program execution steps for n equal to 4, and taking into account that the factorial of number 1 is equal to one, are as follows:

factorial(4) returns 4 × *factorial*(4–1), which is equal to 4 × *factorial*(3);

factorial(3) returns 3 × *factorial*(3–1), which is equal to 3 × *factorial*(2);

factorial(2) returns 2 × *factorial*(2–1), which is equal to 2 × *factorial*(1);

factorial(1) returns 1;

Therefore, the call to the program *factorial*(1) returns the number 1; the call to the program *factorial*(2) returns 2 × 1 = 2; the call to the program *factorial* (3) returns 3 × 2 = 6; and the program *factorial*(3) returns 4 × 6 = 24. On the other hand, in mathematics a recursive function is one that generates its new values from being applied repeatedly on its already known values. For example, the factorial of an n number can be obtained using a recursive mathematical function, which we will name f, such as the following:

$$f(n) = n \times f(n-1)$$

For n equal to four, the result of the function is:

$$f(4) = 4 \times f(3) = 4 \times 3 \times f(2) = 4 \times 3 \times 2 \times f(1) = 4 \times 3 \times 2 \times 1 = 24$$

The interesting thing for us here is that it can be shown that for every Turing machine there is a recursive function. Therefore, in principle, any AE model that is simulated on a computer can be expressed as a set of recursive mathematical formulas, although very complex and not easy to interpret.[4]

---

[4] Strictly speaking, the equivalence is with partial recursive functions. A partial function is that whose domain is a subset of a larger set. For example, a function defined on even natural numbers is a partial function with respect to the set of natural numbers.

For what we have seen so far, we can say that the computational universe and the mathematical universe are not strangers to each other. The mathematical model of a computer is a Turing machine, an algorithm can be thought of as a mathematical function, and a recursive program can be represented with a recursive mathematical function. Moreover, it can be said that computer science, in its theoretical aspects, is part of mathematics. It's just that it is a part that is closer to what is known as constructive mathematics than to classical mathematics.[5]

For constructive mathematics, the proof of the existence of a mathematical object or the demonstration of a theorem must be constructed algorithmically, that is, computationally. The truth, for this approach, must be produced, showing a procedure to reach it. In other words, it must be computable.[6] For classical mathematics this should not always be the case. For example, this is evident in the proofs by contradiction, widely used in the classical approach, but not supported in the constructivist. In such proofs, it is assumed that the object to be produced or the theorem whose truth is to be proved is nonexistent or false, and it is shown that if that were the case, a contradiction would occur. It follows that the object exists, or that the theorem is true. To achieve this result, the principle of the

---

[5] For a discussion on the mathematical nature of the computational models used in AE, see Epstein (2006) and Borrill and Tesfatsion (2010).

[6] K. Vela Velupillai is the founding father of the field known as computable economics. This field investigates the effects on the formulation of economic hypothesis of considering that not everything can be computed because of problems of tractability (algorithmic complexity) or computability. This is particularly interesting since tractability and computability are problematic in full rationality, general equilibrium, and Nash equilibrium models, that is, in many ME models. A problem is intractable if the time to run the program (the algorithm) to solve it grows exponentially as the number of inputs to the problem increases. Computability is the ability to solve a problem in an effective manner by a computing device, in other words, by an algorithm. More precisely, in computability theory, the Church-Turing thesis (due to the work of Alan Turing and Alonzo Church) states that a function on the natural numbers can be calculated by an effective method if and only if it is computable by a Turing machine. Other famous results of computability theory that also have implications for the assumption of full rationality are the Turing halting problem and Kurt Gödel's incompleteness theorems. The Turing halting problem is the problem of determining, from a description of an arbitrary computer program and an input, whether the program will finish running, or continue to run forever, a problem that Turing showed is undecidable. Gödel incompleteness theorems concern the limits of provability in formal axiomatic theories. Roughly speaking, Gödel proved that any set of foundational axioms for mathematics able to describe the natural numbers and arithmetic will be incomplete, since there will always be true sentences about numbers that cannot be proved by those axioms, and that no candidate set of axioms can ever prove its own consistency. For an introduction to computable economics, see Zambelli (2012), and for a wide coverage of the field, see Velupillai, Zambelli, and Kinsella (2012). For a review of the algorithmic complexity of computing economic equilibria, see Roughgarden (2010).

excluded middle is used, which states that a proposition must necessarily be true or false. This principle is not accepted by the constructivist approach, precisely because it can be used in proofs by contradiction which, while capable of establishing the existence of a mathematical object, or the truth of a theorem, do not provide any procedure for the computation (i.e., for the construction), of it.[7]

While, as we have seen, computer science is, in its theoretical aspects, part of mathematics, a question of the universality of ME mathematical models and results versus the ad hoc – or particular – nature of AE computational models and results is usually raised. Indeed, the simulation of an AE model always starts from a given set of initial conditions and parametric values. Therefore, the dynamic that is generated usually changes when those conditions and values change. In contrast, mathematical models of ME are usually formulated and sometimes solved analytically, so that the results obtained are general, in the sense that they do not depend on particular values of parameters or initial conditions or even, sometimes, on the form of the specific mathematical functions that could be used to represent the behavior of agents.

Three observations are pertinent here. First, many of ME mathematical models do not have an analytical solution, so they must be solved with computational numerical methods (i.e., for specific parametric values and initial conditions). Second, there are economic processes, particularly those that generate evolutionary or complex disequilibrium dynamics, for which there are usually no mathematical instruments to model them, so computational simulation is the only alternative way to study their behavior. The lack of such instruments would partly explain ME propensity to focus on the study of equilibrium phenomena, for which there are instruments from classical mathematics that allow them to be modeled. Third, the growing power of computers makes it possible to perform simulations of a model for a very large number of parametric values and initial conditions. In many cases, this allows performance of a very good exploration of the space of its possible dynamics, covering it almost completely, as an analytical solution would if it could be obtained.

Anyway, when contrasting the methodological and instrumental differences between AE and ME, we should not lose sight of the fact that, in

---

[7] For an analysis of the distinction between constructive mathematics and classical mathematics, see Bridges and Palmgren (2018). For discussions of the relationship between constructive mathematics and computer programming, see Martin-Löf (1984) and Bridges and Reeves (1997).

practice, those who deal with one or the other can enrich each other. Economists trained in ME can benefit from computational simulations like the ones used in AE, as they provide the opportunity to create artificial economies to be used as laboratories to "test" theories through controlled virtual experiments, or to suggest, in an exploratory way, ideas or hypotheses that could then be mathematically formalized. Furthermore, gaining more familiarity with the "computational thinking" would allow them to expand their theoretical horizon beyond the universe of full rationality and equilibrium, and their instrumental universe beyond classical mathematical techniques. This will provide them with a deeper appreciation of the scope and limitations of the assumption of full rationality, and will allow them to explore transitional dynamics from one equilibrium to another and, eventually, evolutionary and complex dynamics. Economists working in AE should be aware that sometimes economic theorems or preexisting mathematical models can save them many hours of work, contributing to efficiently guide their computational simulation efforts.[8]

---

[8] For a discussion of how computational simulation and mathematical formalization can be used together to understand the dynamics of computational models, see Izquierdo et al. (2013).

PART II

COMPLEMENTARY TOPICS AND DISCUSSIONS

This second part introduces concepts, models, and discussions that deepen or complement topics presented in Part I. In each chapter, concepts are presented and illustrated with artificial models, and the relationship between concepts with long-standing issues in economics, social sciences, and philosophy, is discussed. Chapter 5, on artificial intelligence, delves into the artificial agent introduced in Chapter 1 through examples of methods of machine learning (unsupervised learning, supervised learning, and reinforcement learning) and discusses themes of philosophy of mind that are naturally linked to the field of artificial intelligence. Chapter 6, on artificial evolution, further analyzes the mechanics of genetic algorithms introduced in Chapter 3, and the evolutionary processes of artificial economies introduced in Chapter 2; presents the concept of evolution as used in the science of evolution; and discusses its uses in economics. Chapter 7, on artificial complexity, presents the concept of a cellular automaton as a simple tool for the generation of complex artificial dynamics; illustrates it with one- and two-dimensional models; introduces basic concepts of the science of complexity; and discusses its uses in economics. Finally, Chapter 8, on the agent/structure problem, discusses how individualist/reductionist, structuralist/holist, and intermediate positions within the social sciences and economics address this problem, and presents guidelines on how to address it through EA methods and models.

5

Artificial Intelligence

In Chapter 1, we introduced the concept of the artificial agent and had reviewed the way contemporary science approaches the phenomenon of intelligence. We emphasized that there are two main approaches to the functional architecture of mental phenomena: one based on sequential rules of the type "if, then" and another based on connectionism (i.e., artificial neural networks). And we saw elementary examples of both types of architectures.

In Chapters 2 and 3, we have seen various types of artificial agents act in different contexts. In Chapter 2, we saw how they explored their environment, moved, and participated in market exchanges, with the goal of achieving the greatest possible accumulation of resources or the maximization of their well-being. In Chapter 3, we observed how they played games, deploying and mutating strategies. These agents showed different forms of artificial intelligence: in some cases, they were simpleminded, while in other cases they had a representation of their reality (of their environment and of their neighbors), and made sophisticated decisions.

In this chapter, we delve into the topic of artificial intelligence, focusing on some of ways of learning of the artificial economic agents. That is, within the field of artificial intelligence, which also includes perception processes, forms of knowledge representation, and other issues, we focus on what is known as machine learning, where these machines are artificial agents. We present methods of unsupervised learning, supervised learning, and reinforcement learning.[1] After that, we explore some links that can be established between artificial intelligence and the philosophy of mind.

---

[1] For a comprehensive introduction to artificial intelligence, see Poole and Mackworth (2017) and Russell and Norvig (2018). For a systematic introduction to machine learning methods, see Alpaydin (2014). For a review of various modeling methods of learning in economics, see Brenner (2006).

5.1 Machine Learning Methods

There are various methods of machine learning, and a common way of classifying them is according to their degree of supervision, or feedback. An unsupervised method is one in which there is no external entity that provides the artificial agent with indications regarding its performance in its learning process. In contrast, in supervised learning the artificial agent receives external indications regarding its advancement in the knowledge of the process it tries to learn. Finally, in reinforcement learning the agent tries to optimally achieve a goal (such as maximizing a benefit or minimizing a cost) while actively interacting with its environment, which it knows partially or even very little.

5.2 Unsupervised Learning

In unsupervised learning, the agent does not have any external entity (a supervisor) that provides information regarding the progress of its learning. A typical case is one in which, given a dataset, the agent must discover whether there are different groups or categories in it. Among the many applications of this type of learning, we can mention the segmentation of consumers in different categories and, outside economics, image recognition, document classification, and genetic groupings.

Remember the Sugarscape model seen in Chapter 2. In that model we had many agents distributed in a grid. Suppose an agent wants to classify all the agents located in a grid of 10×10 cells into different groups, defining a group as a set of agents that are placed "close" to each other. Therefore, for the formation of groups, the concept of distance is crucial. Suppose the agents to be grouped are distributed according to the grid shown in Figure 5.1, and numbered from 1 to 9.

Figure 5.2 displays three successive groupings of agents according to the distance between them. For a distance (horizontal, and/or vertical, and/or diagonal) of at most one cell between any pair of agents, five groups are formed: {1}, {2,3,4}, {5,6}, {7,8}, and {9}. If we increase the distance to at most four cells, we have three groups consisting of {1}, {2,3,4,5,6}, and {7,8,9}. And finally, if we increase the distance to at most ten cells, we have a single group made up of all the agents.

The example just seen is extremely simple: agents are grouped according to a geographical distance between them. If we remember that in the Sugarscape each agent, in addition to a position on the grid, had a level of metabolism and a vision range, we could build groupings according to the

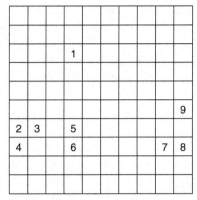

Figure 5.1 Agents, numbered from 1 to 9, distributed on a grid of 10 × 10 cells

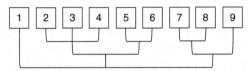

Figure 5.2 Agent grouping tree according to specific distances between each other

distance in each of these characteristics. That is, we could group agents with similar levels of metabolism, or vision. From what we see, the concept of distance does not come down to that of conventional geographical distance.[2]

Grouping agents by a geographic distance, or in groups of similar vision or metabolism, could be useful for an artificial agent with some sophistication. For example, this agent could classify other agents' trade behavior according to the group they belong to, then optimize its exchange strategies with them.

5.3 Supervised Learning

In supervised learning the artificial agent receives indications from a supervisor (an external mechanism). For example, given an input (a dataset) and an output (another dataset), the agent must best approximate the process that transforms the input into outputs, so that, given an input, it can predict the corresponding output. The process is as follows: given an

---

[2] What is commonly known as distance, and which we applied in the example, is the Euclidean distance. But there are other measures of distance, such as the maximum distance, the Manhattan distance, and the Mahalanobis distance, which can also be applied in grouping algorithms.

input, the agent generates (predicts) an output. A supervisor, who knows the operation of the environment in which the agent operates, shows it the correct output that corresponds to the received input. The agent computes the error made, measuring the difference between its output and the correct one, and adjusts the components of its prediction process in order to generate the correct output. The process is repeated for a set of inputs and outputs that is provided to the agent by the supervisor, until the agent learns reasonably well to predict the correct outputs.

The applications of this type of learning are broad and varied, and analogous to those of statistical and econometric analysis: for example, given data on population, age, sex, income level, etc., consumers' behavior can be predicted; given data on technology, wages, and input costs, firms' behavior can be predicted; etc.

Remember now the evolutionary game presented in Chapter 3. In this game, the strategy of each agent was contained in a chromosome represented by a binary string (i.e., a sequence of zeros and ones), where each number represented an action: one to cooperate, and zero to defect. These agents were very rudimentary, as they always repeated the same strategy, as it was recorded on their chromosomes. They didn't learn anything.

Let's assume now that we have an agent that is a little more sophisticated and can learn. And that it wants to be able to predict what action its opponent will take, given the actions it took in the past. More specifically, suppose that our agent has access, through some external mechanism (a supervisor), to the history of the last four actions of its opponent, and that they follow a pattern like this:

1110

which means that its opponent, after cooperating three times in a row, defects. Let's assume that our agent is equipped with an artificial neural network like the one introduced in Chapter 1. In this case, as shown in Figure 5.3, it is an extremely simple neural network: it only has a layer of three input nodes, a hidden node, and a single output node, which allows the agent to learn the behavior of its opponent, and therefore predict it.

The artificial neural network works as follows: it receives stimuli from the input node layer (in this case, three numbers one) which feed, in our simple example, a hidden node. In the hidden node there is a combination function that computes the net value of the stimuli. And an activation function that determines, comparing the value of the net stimulus to a given threshold, whether the output node is activated or not.

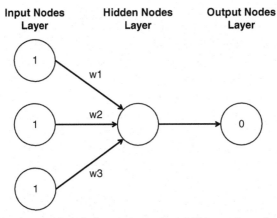

Figure 5.3 Neural network with three input nodes, a hidden node, and an output node

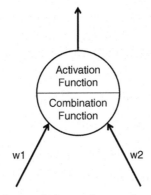

Figure 5.4 Node of a neural network that receives two input stimuli and generates one output

The combination function receives stimuli, either from the input node layer or from other nodes in the hidden layer (if there is more than one) and computes a value that represents the intensity of the net stimulus. Usually such a computation is performed as the weighted sum of the stimuli received.

For example, in Figure 5.4 we see a node that receives two stimuli, say stimuli one and two. The combination function is equal to the sum of the product of the w1 weight multiplied by the value of stimulus one, plus the product of the w2 weight multiplied by the value of stimulus two.

The activation function generates the response given the net stimulus received by the node and computed by the combination function.[3] This is sometimes done using a threshold function to determine when the node should trigger a response, which occurs when the activation function generates a value above that threshold.

The learning process in an artificial neural network happens through the change in weights (i.e., the values of the w's). Therefore, in this context, learning is to adjust the values of the weights of each stimulus on each node, so that the overall response of the network is the right one. For this to happen the network must have been previously trained and learned to generate the right responses.

Therefore, we can think that the values of the weights in an artificial neural network that has already been trained form a structure that directs the flow of stimuli within the network, so that it generates the correct output responses given a set of input stimuli.

In our simple example of a neural network with three input nodes, one hidden, and one output node, the combination function is the weighted sum of the three received stimuli, where w1, w2, and w3 are the weights, and gives us the value of the net stimulus:

net stimulus = w1 × stimulus 1 + w2 × stimulus 2 + w3 × stimulus 3

while the activation function operates according to the following rule:

if net stimulus is > threshold, then fire a 1

if net stimulus is ≤ threshold, then fire a 0

The learning or training process of this neural network is as follows. Given the values of the three input stimuli which, in our example, are: (1,1,1); the value of the corresponding output response (in our example, zero); and the value of an activation threshold (which we will assume to be equal to one), we must calculate the value that the weights w1, w2, and w3 should have so that, each time the stimuli (1,1,1) are received as inputs, a response equal to zero is fired.

A very simple procedure for calculating weights is the following iterative process. We start with a set of three arbitrary values for the weights, for example:

---

[3] A node's response is usually constrained to be within the [0,1] interval, using a variety of functional forms for the activation function.

$$w1 = 0.4 \qquad w2 = 0.1 \qquad w3 = 0.9$$

Given these weights, and the values of the input stimuli, we compute the net value of the activation function:

$$1.4 = 0.4 \times 1 + 0.1 \times 1 + 0.9 \times 1$$

Since 1.4 is greater than the activation threshold of the output node (which we set equal to one), then the output node will fire a one. If we compare this value with the desired value that should be fired (a value equal to zero), we see that they are different. Therefore, we need to update the weights. To make this update, we proceed as follows:

$$w.new = w.previous + \alpha \times (\text{desired value} - \text{fired value}) \times \text{input stimulus}$$

That is, the new value of each weight is computed from its previous value. To this we add a coefficient α (named learning rate, to which we arbitrarily give the value 0.1) multiplied by the prediction error (the difference between the correct or desired value, and that fired by the neural network), multiplied in turn by the input stimulus. If we apply this formula to our example, we get:

$$w1.new = 0.4 + 0.1 \times (0 - 1) \times 1 = 0.3$$
$$w2.new = 0.1 + 0.1 \times (0 - 1) \times 1 = 0.0$$
$$w3.new = 0.9 + 0.1 \times (0 - 1) \times 1 = 0.8$$

With these new weights we recompute the value of the activation function and get:

$$1.1 = 0.3 \times 1 + 0.0 \times 1 + 0.8 \times 1$$

This value is greater than 1, the value of the trigger threshold of the output node, so that the fired response will be again equal to one, and therefore different from the correct one. If we apply the procedure for updating the value of the weights again, we get:

$$w1.new = 0.3 + 0.1 \times (0 - 1) \times 1 = 0.2$$
$$w2.new = 0.0 + 0.1 \times (0 - 1) \times 1 = -0.1$$
$$w3.new = 0.8 + 0.1 \times (0 - 1) \times 1 = 0.7$$

and the new value of the activation function is:

$$0.8 = 0.2 \times 1 - 0.1 \times 1 + 0.7 \times 1$$

This value is less than the threshold, and therefore the response value will be zero (i.e., the desired or correct value). The neural network has learned to predict correctly. From now on, since the values of the weights will be w1 = 0.2, w2 = −0.1 and w3 = 0.7, each time the neural network receives (1,1,1) as stimuli, it will fire a zero.

We have presented a very simple example, in which we train the neural network to respond correctly to a single pattern of behavior of the opposing player. If we wanted to train the network to respond to other types of behavioral patterns, we should feed it with other examples and continue to update the weights accordingly. The activation function we used was also very simple, while usually, the value of the net stimulus is transformed through some mathematical function (such as those known as sigmoid functions, logistic functions, or other functional forms) before comparing it against the threshold.

Also, the neural network we used was extremely simple: it had only three input nodes, one hidden, and one output node. Of course, such a network could be made of many input nodes, hidden nodes, and output nodes, and, therefore, many weights. Nevertheless, the learning procedure could be thought of as analogous to the one just demonstrated. From a series of multiple sets of input stimuli and the corresponding desired output responses, we would proceed to train the neural network with an iterative process of updating the weights similar, in spirit, to the one we applied in our example. In fact, the most important problem in the process of learning of an artificial neural network is how to modify the values of the weights so that the margin of error is reduced as soon as possible. To achieve this, there are various mathematical optimization methods that can be applied, such as gradient descent, Newton, conjugate gradient, etc. In Annex D we present an introduction to more complex artificial neural networks models and learning methods.

5.4 Reinforcement Learning

In reinforcement learning, the agent seeks to reach a goal optimally (e.g., maximizing a benefit or minimizing a cost) while actively interacting with an environment that it does not know and tries to learn. As shown in Figure 5.5, the agent interacts with the environment through actions, which generate observable reactions that have associated rewards (prizes or punishments, benefits or costs). As it learns the effects of its actions and the corresponding rewards, the agent tries to find the optimal way to act in order to efficiently achieve its goal.[4]

---

[4] For a systematic introduction to reinforcement learning, see Sutton and Barto (2018).

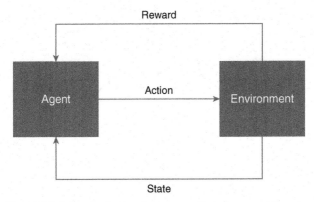

Figure 5.5 Scheme of a simple process of reinforcement learning

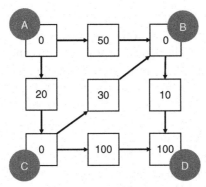

Figure 5.6 A nine-cell grid, with four possible entry cells (A, B, C, or D), and with directions of movement marked with arrows. The numbers indicate the amount of sugar available in each cell

Let us recall again the Sugarscape model that we presented in Chapter 2, in which agents moved on a grid to collect as much as possible of a resource named sugar. In that model, each agent had a vision range that determined the limits of its neighborhood. And we assumed it knew its neighborhood, that is, how much sugar was in each cell. Let's assume now the agent's neighborhood consists of nine cells like the ones we can see in Figure 5.6, and that it can only move from one cell to another according to the direction of the arrows.

The numbers indicate the amount of sugar in each cell. We will also assume that the agent can only enter the neighborhood from cells A, B, C, or D, and if it wishes it can stop at them. And that, for the rest of the cells, it

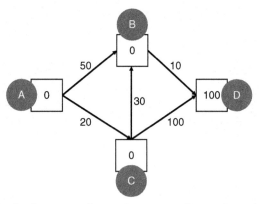

Figure 5.7 Graph of actions and rewards, corresponding to the grid in Figure 5.6

can only pass and collect the available sugar. For example, if it is in cell A, it can move to cell B and on the way collect the 50 units of sugar available in the intermediate cell. The agent's possible actions and the corresponding rewards are represented in the graph shown in Figure 5.7.

Our agent's goal is to collect as much sugar as possible. Therefore, it must determine an optimal sequence of actions that lead it down the best possible path. The most commonly used methods to solve this problem are those that compute the value of each action and select those actions whose value is as high as possible, in order to build an optimal sequence of actions. To build this sequence, an evaluation function is usually applied that, as we shall see, relates the values of successive actions.

Depending on the amount of information the agent has access to, there are various methods to solve the problem. We will analyze two cases: perfect information and almost zero information. The last case is the one of reinforcement learning, while the first one we present is an introductory step.

Let's assume that the agent has perfect information, that is, a complete knowledge of the "model" of his neighborhood, and thus does not face any uncertainty. To solve the problem, it will apply a method known as dynamic programming. Dynamic programming simplifies a complicated problem by separating it into simpler and smaller subproblems; and these smaller subproblems are recursively nested within the larger ones. The method deals with a sequence of actions from back to front, computing the optimal value of each by means of an evaluation function known as the Bellman equation (developed by mathematician Richard Bellman in the late 1950s) which has the form:

$$V_t(s) = \max [R_t(s, a) + V_{t+1}(s')]$$

We see that the V value of being in the s state (in the case of our agent, of being in a cell of its neighborhood) in period t, is equal to the maximum of the sum of two components. The first component is equal to the reward R obtained for taking, in period t, the action a of moving from state s to the next state s'. The second component is the value of V in period t+1 in the next state s'. Since from a given state the agent can move to more than one next state, and therefore has at its disposal more than one possible action, it must choose the sum $[R_t (s,a) + V_{t+1}(s')]$ that gives it the maximum value.[5]

Remember that the agent wants to maximize the amount of sugar collected in its neighborhood, according to the graph of actions and rewards represented in Figure 5.7 graph. Thus, it will proceed as follows (for simplicity, we omit the t subscripts). First, it computes the terminal state value, which corresponds to state D, that is, the value of being in cell D. This value is measured as the amount of sugar collected, and it is equal to:

$$V(D) = 100$$

Next, it computes the value of being in state B, that is, the value of being in cell B and from it to be able to move to another state (another cell). In this case, it is something very simple as there is only one possible move: to go from B to D. The application of the evaluation function yields:

$$V(B) = \max[R(B, D) + V(D)]$$
$$= \max[10 + 100]$$
$$= 110$$

The optimal path is obviously (B,D). Next, it computes the value of the C state. In this case there is more than one possible path that departs from C. Applying the evaluation function:

$$V(C) = \max[R(C, D) + V(D); R(C, B) + V(B)]$$
$$= \max[100 + 100; 30 + 110]$$
$$= \max[200; 140]$$
$$= 200$$

---

[5] The Bellman equation may contain a time discount factor δ, which measures the relative value of present rewards with respect to future rewards. This factor is included in the equation multiplying the term $V(s')$. In order to present as simple an example as possible, we assume that δ is equal to 1.

The optimal path to go from C to D is (C,D). Next it computes the value of A. To do this it will apply again the evaluation function, getting:

$$V(A) = \max[R(A, B) + V(B); R(A, C) + V(C)]$$
$$= \max[50 + 110; 20 + 200]$$
$$= \max[160; 220]$$
$$= 220$$

The optimal path to take when the agent is in A, is to go from A to C. And since the optimal path to take when it is in C is to go toward D, then the optimal path to go from A to D is (A,C), (C,D).

Let's assume now that the agent doesn't have information about its neighborhood, beyond that there are four cells (A, B, C, and D) from which it can enter. In this case, it must learn the entire model of its neighborhood through its actions, observing what effects they produce and what rewards they generate. This is a typical situation of reinforcement learning. In the following we will introduce a method of reinforcement learning known as Q-learning.

With this method, the agent seeks to determine the maximum value of each of its possible actions. To do this, it will gradually store information about those values in a reward table (which we will call Q). The rows in the table indicate the cells where the agent is, and the columns the cells toward which it can move. For example, the expression Q(B,D) = 110 means that the value of being in cell B and taking the action of going from there to cell D is equal to 110. As shown in Table 5.1, initially all values in the table are equal to zero, since the agent knows almost nothing about its neighborhood.

Our agent's basic rule of learning is the following evaluation function, which is somewhat like the Bellman equation seen previously:

$$Q(s, a) = R(s, a) + \max[Q(s', a')]$$

The Q value of taking the action a in state s, is equal to the sum of two components. The first component is equal to the reward R obtained for taking action a in state s. The second component is the maximum value of Q that can be obtained in the next state s', from the possible actions a'.[6] Let's then start

---

[6] The general Q-learning evaluation function is:

$$Q\text{-new}(s, a) = (1 - \alpha) \times Q\text{-old}(s, a) + \alpha \times [R(s, a) + \delta \times \max[Q(s', a')]]$$

where α is a learning rate parameter that controls how much of the difference between a new Q value and an old Q value is considered. In order to present the simplest possible

Table 5.1 *Q-learning initial reward table*

	A	B	C	D
A	0	0	0	0
B	0	0	0	0
C	0	0	0	0
D	0	0	0	0

Table 5.2 *Q-learning reward table first update*

	A	B	C	D
A	0	0	0	0
B	0	0	0	0
C	0	0	0	0
D	0	0	0	100

applying the Q-learning algorithm to our case. Remember the graph presented in Figure 5.7; that the agent knows almost nothing about its neighborhood; and that it can get into it through any of the four cells: A, B, C, or D.

Suppose it enters the neighborhood through cell D. There it learns that it can collect 100 units of sugar, and that it can't go anywhere else, finishing the tour. Applying the evaluation function, it obtains simply:

$$Q(D) = R(D, D)$$
$$= 100$$

Therefore, in the Q table, the agent gives the element (D,D) a value of 100, as shown in Table 5.2.

Now let's suppose that the agent enters the neighborhood through cell B. There it learns that it only has one possible action: go from B to D, collecting ten units of sugar on the way, and then stay in D, collecting 100 more units and finishing the tour. Applying the evaluation function, it obtains:

$$Q(B, D) = R(B, D) + Q(D, D)$$
$$110 = 10 + 100$$

example, in our case we made $\delta = 1$ and $\alpha = 1$. The latter makes the difference between the Q-old and Q-new terms disappear, so in our example we simply use Q(s,a).

Table 5.3 *Q-learning reward table second update*

	A	B	C	D
A	0	0	0	0
B	0	0	0	110
C	0	0	0	0
D	0	0	0	100

Table 5.4 *Q-learning reward table third update*

	A	B	C	D
A	0	0	0	0
B	0	0	0	110
C	0	140	0	0
D	0	0	0	100

So, in the Q table, the agent gives the (B,D) element a value equal to 110, as shown in Table 5.3.

Now let's suppose that the agent enters the neighborhood through cell C. There it learns that it has two possible actions: go to cell B, or go to cell D. Suppose it randomly chooses to go to B. Then it learns that from cell B it can go to the D cell and finally stay there, finishing the tour. Applying the evaluation function, it obtains:

$$Q(C, B) = R(C, B) + \max[Q(B, D)]$$
$$140 = 30 + 110$$

which is a trivial case of choosing a maximum, since there is only one Q value to choose from. In the reward table the agent gives the element (C,B) a value of 140, as shown in Table 5.4.

Now let's suppose that the agent enters the neighborhood through cell A. There it learns that it has two possible actions: go to cell B, or go to cell C. Suppose it randomly chooses to go to C. Then it learns that from cell C it can go to cell B or to cell D. Applying the evaluation function the agent obtains:

$$Q(A, C) = R(A, C) + \max[Q(C, B), Q(C, D)]$$
$$160 = 20 + \max[140, 0] = 20 + 140$$

Table 5.5 *Q-learning reward table fourth update*

	A	B	C	D
A	0	0	160	0
B	0	0	0	110
C	0	140	0	0
D	0	0	0	100

Table 5.6 *Q-learning final reward table*

	A	B	C	D
A	0	160	220	0
B	0	0	0	110
C	0	140	0	200
D	0	0	0	100

In the reward table the agent gives the (A,C) element a value of 160, and moves toward cell B. Once in cell B, it learns that it has only one possible action, which is to go to cell D, collect 100 units of sugar, and finish the tour. The case is identical to the one we saw previously, and that will not alter the value of the (B,D) element in the reward table, which will remain equal to 110, as shown in Table 5.5.

If the agent continues the procedure for the other possible neighborhood tour cases, and if it also repeats the various possible routes starting randomly from the different entry cells, it will eventually get the values of the reward table converge toward a stable set like the one shown in Table 5.6.

This Q-learning table gives the agent all the information it needs to perform optimally, starting from any cell. For example, if it is in cell A, it only needs to examine the corresponding row of the table and choose the action with the highest Q value (i.e., 220). Therefore, whenever it is in cell A, its optimal action will be to go to cell C. If it is in cell B, its optimal action will be to go to D. If it is in C, it must go to D. And if it is in D, it will have to stay there.

We have seen two cases: one with perfect information and one with near-zero information regarding the model of the neighborhood where the artificial agent had to move to achieve its goal of collecting as much sugar as possible. There are intermediate cases, in which the information is partial, leading to different forms and degrees of uncertainty. These cases can be posed as problems that are solved with stochastic control methods. These methods are widely used in the field of economics to model and solve various types of problems of dynamic optimization of decisions under uncertainty. Notions on stochastic control are provided in Annex E.

5.5 Artificial Agents and Philosophy of Mind

We can think of each of the learning methods presented in the previous section as typical of different types of artificial agents. Or we can also see them as methods used by a single agent. Indeed, in order to achieve a given goal, a sophisticated artificial agent should group the component elements of its environment (unsupervised learning), make predictions about their behavior (supervised learning), and actively interact with them (reinforcement learning). If we deal with an artificial agent with these characteristics, could we infer that it is intelligent, or even more so, that it thinks?

If we define intelligence as we did earlier, such as the ability to represent, learn, and make decisions based on goals, we should recognize that the agent is intelligent. As for whether it is capable of thinking, the question becomes more difficult, since it is often assumed that thought is a typically human quality. To sort this out, we can resort to the famous Turing test. In mid-twentieth century, Alan Turing proposed a very simple test: if we ask numerous questions of any kind to a hidden interlocutor (which is actually an artificial agent) and, after getting the answers, we cannot determine whether we are talking to a person or to an artificial agent, we should conclude that our interlocutor (the artificial agent) is able to think as a person does.[7] Can we also conclude that that agent has a mental life or, moreover, a subjectivity? Here things get even more complicated, and they take us to the realm of what is known as philosophy of mind.

There are two main paradigms of philosophy of mind: continental philosophy of mind, named in this way for having its predominance in continental Europe; and analytical or Anglo-Saxon philosophy of mind, so called because it predominates in English-speaking countries.[8]

Continental philosophy of mind is considered as subjectivist, because it focuses on the meaning attributed to people's behavior, and on qualitative analysis with interpretive and hermeneutic methods. It is often said that from this paradigm "the world is seen in the first-person perspective." Within this philosophy stands out the current of thought named phenomenology which, starting from the work of Edmund Husserl at the beginning

---

[7] The classic work is Turing (1950). For a review of the discussions on the Turing test in the fifty years following its publication, see Saygin, Cicekli, and Akman (2000).

[8] For an accessible and broad introduction to philosophy of mind see Lowe (2000).

of the twentieth century, and continued by his followers during the twentieth and even the twenty-first century, gives a fundamental role to introspective individual experience.

Anglo-Saxon philosophy of mind is considered as objectivist, since it focuses on behavior as instrumental action, and on the analysis of it with analytical, mathematical, and computational methods. It is often said that from this paradigm "the world is seen in the third-person perspective," which corresponds to the canonical paradigm of contemporary science.

Within Anglo-Saxon philosophy of mind there are several positions, among which two stand out: eliminativism and functionalism. Eliminativism, with prominent figures such as Patricia and Paul Churchland, considers that mental phenomena as they are usually conceived do not exist, since they are non-scientific concepts of folk psychology that will be abandoned as science advances, as it happened with the concept of phlogiston in chemistry, or with the concepts from astrology and demonology. And that the only thing that exists are structures and brain functions, that is, material neurological states.

Functionalism has in its ranks prominent figures such as Hilary Putnam and Jerry Fodor. It considers that mental phenomena are functions (something like the software) of the brain or any other physical medium that allows reproduction of them. This is the main stance of cognitive science, which we introduced in Chapter 1, and pretty much the one of AE. Within functionalism, there is in turn a reductionist stance that argues that mental phenomena could and eventually will be completely reduced to physical phenomena, and a non-reductionist one, for which mental phenomena are emergent properties of the brain. For this posture, the brain is neither a necessary condition for the existence of the mind (since this one could have other types of material supports) nor a sufficient condition (because there will always be an irreducible residue as far as mental phenomena are concerned regarding its material support). In other words, for emergentism, mental phenomena are a qualitatively distinct property that emerges from the functioning of its material base, but can't be reduced to it.[9]

There are several philosophical critiques to functionalism and its view of the mind as a generic processor of information. Even within Anglo-Saxon philosophy of mind there are critiques from a perspective that might be considered as a vindication of subjectivity. They focus on the fact that functionalism presents a purely relational characterization of mental states,

---

[9] Chapter 7, when dealing with the science of complexity, presents an introductory discussion of emergentism.

without saying anything about what their "intrinsic" properties are supposed to be. Such criticisms take the form of various arguments, usually developed through mental experiments.

One of these arguments is the so-called *qualia* problem, which refers to the subjective qualities of personal experiences. This problem has been analyzed by, among others, Thomas Nagel, who emphasized that there are facts regarding conscious experience that can only be experienced from a subjective perspective. For example, even if we knew all the objective facts about bats, we could never really know "what it's like to be" a bat. And by David Chalmers in the problem of philosophical zombies, hypothetical beings who would be physically indistinguishable from a human, but devoid of subjectivity or first-person experiences. For example, they would react in the same way as a human when taking a hit, but without feeling pain; or to good news, but without feeling joy.

Also noteworthy is the argument developed by John Searle and known as the problem of meaning, or the Chinese room argument. In this problem, it is assumed that a person who does not speak the Chinese language, locked in a room, and provided with an algorithm (a set of rules) to link Chinese symbols, receives as inputs questions (sequences of Chinese symbols) and after querying her algorithm, returns as outputs answers (another set of Chinese symbols). For an external observer, the person inside the room understands the Chinese language, but that person does not really know anything about Chinese, and therefore does not understand the meaning of the symbols she manipulates.[10]

Other critiques of functionalism can be linked to some aspects of the thought of Martin Heidegger and Ludwig Wittgenstein, two of the most influential and controversial philosophers of the twentieth century, who carried out a critical analysis of the conventional way of conceiving a subject's situation in the world, and of the conventional separation between subject and object. According to Charles Taylor (1995), in both philosophers there is a critique of the possibility of conceiving a subject who is disembodied or disassociated from her physical and contextual social world. On the contrary, the way of living and experiencing the world is that of a subject who has a body, is part of a specific social situation, and is immersed within the universe of a language. Therefore, it would be a mistake to think of the mind as something disembodied,

---

[10] For a presentation and discussion of the qualia, the philosophical zombies, and the Chinese room arguments see, respectively, Tye (2018), Kirk (2019), and Cole (2020).

disassociated, and unsocialized, as if it were a generic processor of information.[11]

Heidegger claims, in *Being and Time* (Heidegger, 2008), that things are always discovered as part of a world, within which they are interrelated with other things. Moreover, subjects are always thinking and acting on a background, of which they are not fully aware and could not be, but which is the implicit condition of pre-understanding of their actions, and makes their experiences intelligible to them. While Wittgenstein, in *Philosophical Investigations* (Wittgenstein, 2016), argues that it is naive to believe that the meaning of a word (its ostensive definition) stems from the fact that it names or means an object. On the contrary, that definition is intelligible only if the subject understands in advance the games of language in which she is immersed, and the place that word occupies within the multiple relationships that occur within that language.[12]

It seems that Wittgenstein and Heidegger somehow refer to the existence of tacit knowledge that cannot be coded. While classical cognitive science–based artificial intelligence operates by coding knowledge and processing it through explicit formal rules, the existence of tacit knowledge in humans would be an impediment for computers or robots to emulate their behavior completely, given the impossibility of transferring such knowledge in a coded manner. Hubert Dreyfus, drawing from Heidegger's philosophy, raised arguments like these almost since the beginning of the work on artificial intelligence in the 1950s and 1960s. Dreyfus argued that human intelligence depends more on unconscious processes than on the conscious manipulation of symbols by algorithmic rules, and that such unconscious processes or abilities could never be captured by formal rules such as those used in classical cognitive science. Dreyfus raised his criticisms in a famous book entitled *What Computers Can't Do: A Criticism of Artificial Reason* (Dreyfus, 1972). However, twenty years later he published a new edition entitled *What Computers Still Can't Do* (Dreyfus, 1992), nuancing his positions in view of the advances in the fields of cognitive science and artificial intelligence, which began to work, in addition to rules-based architectures, with connectionist architectures. Also, for many researchers in the field of artificial intelligence, tacit knowledge would not be an impediment for computers or robots to emulate

---

[11] Notice that this is reminiscent of the embodied and embedded approach to cognitive science we presented in Chapter 1.

[12] In this vein, and from a social theory perspective, Theodore Schatzki develops a theory of practice based on Wittgenstein's and Heidegger's thinking, in which practices determine the subjects' horizon of intelligibility. See Schatzki (1996 and 2002).

human behavior, since they could do it albeit through processes of acquiring and processing knowledge other than that of humans, so they would not need a tacit knowledge transfer.[13]

Finally, it is worth mentioning that the scientific and technical advances in artificial intelligence, biotechnology, and genetic engineering lead, for some thinkers, to question humanism as a philosophy concerning the human condition. This is due to the radical transformation that such advances could entail at the level of the physical and mental capacities of individuals (in terms of health, longevity, strength, beauty, intelligence, memory, feelings, etc.) giving rise to different life forms than those we traditionally associate with human life, whether in the form of a new species, of organisms with cybernetic and organic components (cyborgs), or even of intelligent entities without a biological support. This is the stance of what is known as transhumanism, a kind of Neo-Darwinist philosophy or view of the world that, with a high degree of confidence in the benefits of technological change, suggests that humans should take evolution into their own hands and direct it through technology.[14]

Various utopias and dystopias have been derived from this position regarding future transhuman individuals and their possible, probable, and desirable forms of economic and social organization. It is an interesting challenge to see to what extent the concepts and methods of AE, and even of ME, would be applicable in human-transhuman economic relations, or in transhuman forms of economic organization, and if they could contribute to bringing order to reasoning sometimes based more on science fiction literature than on scientific analysis. Problems of scarcity and allocation of resources, optimization and planning under uncertainty, design of efficient economic institutions (rules of the economic game), and simulation of various forms of economic interaction are likely to remain as valid as they are today, and thus be useful in addressing issues regarding the economic relationships between humans and transhumans, or to study "transhuman economics."

---

[13] For an argument along these lines, see Prawitz (1990). For a broad discussion of the concept of tacit knowledge, see Turner (2015).

[14] For presentations and discussions of transhumanist arguments, see Ranish and Sorgner (2014) and Harari (2017).

6

Artificial Evolution

The study of biological evolutionary processes found its masterful formulation in the mid-nineteenth century in Charles Darwin's theory of natural selection. Since then, applications of this theory have been made in the field of social sciences and economics. More recently, advancement in hardware and software technologies made it possible for AE to simulate evolutionary processes with powerful computational instruments. Among these are genetic algorithms, such as those we saw in the evolutionary game of Chapter 3, and models of artificial markets such as the one we saw in Chapter 2. In what follows, we delve into the evolutionary dynamics of genetic algorithms and artificial markets. Then we introduce basic concepts of the theory of evolution and discuss some of its main applications in economics.

6.1 Genetic Algorithms and Extrinsic Adaptation

In Chapter 3, we applied a genetic algorithm in the context of an evolutionary game. Genetic algorithms are one of the most popular computational instruments for modeling and simulating evolutionary processes. There are different kinds of genetic algorithms, and here we succinctly present one of the most common.[1] The genetic algorithm consists of an iterative procedure that, starting from an initial population, evaluates its adaptation, selects and crosses over some of its most adapted members, and replaces the old population with a new generation.

Assume that, as shown in Table 6.1, the initial population (generation one) has four members, whose characteristics are represented by a chromosome formed by a string of five binary digits, each digit representing a gene. For each generation, next to the binary expression of each chromosome, we write

---

[1] For a systematic introduction to genetic algorithms, see Mitchell (1996).

Table 6.1 *Initial population*
(generation one) for genetic
algorithms

Binary Value	Decimal Value
0 1 0 0 1	9
1 1 1 0 1	29
1 1 0 1 1	27
0 1 0 1 0	10

its equivalent value in decimal numbers, to facilitate the identification of the numeric value associated with each chromosome.[2]

For selecting the fittest individuals, we need some criteria. A mathematical function, named adaptive or fitness function, is generally used. This function can take various forms. Here we will simply use the two highest numeric values associated with the respective chromosomes. Therefore, in this case, we select the second and third individuals, who have respectively the values 29 and 27. We assume that they will form a couple that will have four children. Each child's chromosome is made from the crossover and mutation of its parents' chromosomes.

In Table 6.2, we illustrate the functioning of two genetic algorithms with minor differences in the chromosome crossover procedure. In genetic algorithm 1 (GA1), the parents' chromosome crossover procedure exchanges the last two genes of each chromosome, while in genetic algorithm 2 (GA2), the third and fourth genes are exchanged. The genes that are exchanged are shown inside a box. This results in two new chromosomes corresponding to the crossover of those of the parents. Then, to obtain the chromosomes of the four children, we assume that a mutation of the last gene of each crossover occurs (i.e., where the value was equal to zero is replaced by a value equal to one, and vice versa). Genes that mutate are shown inside a box. Then, in GA1 the mutation occurs in the fifth gene,

---

[2] Let us remember that in order to obtain the decimal representation of a binary number, each position of the number is multiplied, from right to left, by the corresponding ascending power of the number two. For example, for the binary number 01001 we proceed as follows:

$$0 \times 2^4 + 1 \times 2^3 + 0 \times 2^2 + 0 \times 2^1 + 1 \times 2^0$$
$$= 0 \times 16 + 1 \times 8 + 0 \times 4 + 0 \times 2 + 1 \times 1$$
$$= 0 + 8 + 0 + 0 + 1 = 9$$

Table 6.2 *Generation two as a result of two different genetic algorithms*

GA1			GA2		
Parents	Crossover	Mutation (generation 2)	Parents	Crossover	Mutation (generation 2)
11101	111[11]	1111[1] 31	11101	11[01]1	1101[1] 27
		1111[0] 30			1100[1] 25
11011	110[01]	1100[1] 25	11011	11[10]1	1110[1] 29
		1100[0] 24			1111[1] 31

Table 6.3 *Generation three as a result of two different genetic algorithms*

GA1			GA2		
Parents	Crossover	Mutation (generation 3)	Parents	Crossover	Mutation (generation 3)
11111	111[10]	1111[0] 30	11101	11[11]1	111[1]1 31
		1111[1] 31			111[0]1 29
11110	111[11]	1111[1] 31	11111	11[10]1	111[0]1 29
		1111[0] 30			111[1]1 31

while in GA2 it occurs in the fourth gene. Thus, for GA1 and GA2 we get the corresponding second generation of the population.

As shown in Table 6.3, we select again the two fittest individuals. In the case of GA1, they are the first and the second, as they have the highest numeric values; in GA2, they are the third and fourth. We reapply the crossover and mutation procedure, and get generation three corresponding to GA1 and GA2.

We select again the two fittest individuals. In GA1, they are the second and third; in GA2, the first and fourth. But note that in both algorithms we have reached the highest possible values (i.e., the binary sequence 11111), corresponding to the decimal value 31. From now on, if we continue to apply the genetic algorithms, the generations we obtain will be identical, because we have reached an optimal. We can conclude that a genetic algorithm is an optimization method, that is, a procedure that, for a given problem, allows us to find the best possible value.

This simple example can be modified in several ways, as is done in the field of genetic algorithms. We could start from a much larger initial population, or use longer chromosomes. We can use a more complex adaptive function than simply selecting the maximum value. We can select more than one couple of parents, and do so using random processes. Instead of having fixed crossover and mutation points, their location within the chromosome sequence might be randomly selected; even the sequence of genes corresponding to the crossover and mutations could also be of variable length and randomly selected.

Genetic algorithms are very powerful optimization methods. However, it is not yet known for sure what their power is based on. They are supposed to operate by discovering and recombining good building blocks (pieces of chromosomes called schemes) of the best candidates obtained at each step. But this is still a very active area of research.

In most genetic algorithms, adaptation values are assigned to candidate solutions – that is, to the chromosomes – independently of each other. Thus, chromosomes only interact through their competition by selection places within the fitness function, which is given extrinsically, as we saw in the previous examples in which the fitness function was simply a maximum value function. Therefore, adaptation is extrinsic, since there are no eco-logical interactions in the population, which would bring about an intrinsic fitness function, as we will see in the following.[3]

6.2 Artificial Markets and Intrinsic Adaptation

In Chapter 2, we introduced an artificial market model, in which agents lived in a geography collecting and trading two resources (sugar and spice) necessary for their survival. These agents were heterogeneous: their genetic characteristics (vision and metabolism) varied from agent to agent. To survive, an agent had to meet its metabolic needs in each period, otherwise it would die. As time went on, the population decreased, to stabilize at some level where only survivors remained, that is, the agents most adapted to their environment. It should be noted that the environment of each agent was made up of not only the geography of resources, but also of the other agents with which it competed for those resources.

An interesting experiment is to analyze changes in the average genetic characteristics of the population as the evolutionary dynamic unfolds. To this end, we perform a simulation for fifty periods. We start from an initial population of agents with genetic characteristics randomly distributed among them: their metabolic needs of sugar and spice take values between one and five, and vision ranges also vary between one and five. Figure 6.1

---

[3] For an introduction to the concepts of extrinsic and intrinsic adaptation, and a presentation of a simple model of intrinsic artificial evolution, see Packard (1989).

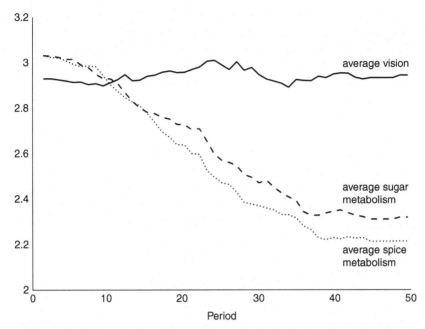

Figure 6.1 Evolution of average population values of vision, of sugar metabolism, and of spice metabolism, over 50 periods

shows the evolution of the average population values of vision, of sugar metabolism, and of spice metabolism.

Both vision and average metabolisms begin with values close to three, and then take divergent paths. As we would expect, in the period-by-period survivor population the average vision tends to grow (as it broadens the search horizon for resources) and the average metabolisms of sugar and spice tend to decrease (because in that way survival becomes easier). However, we can see that average vision does not always grow monotonously, and that the average metabolisms of sugar and spice do not always decrease monotonously, but that there are short periods when average vision decreases, and average metabolisms grow.

Unlike in the genetic algorithms in the previous section, evolutionary dynamic does not depend on an extrinsic fitness function that systematically selects agents with greater vision and lower metabolism. In this case, adaptation is intrinsically generated as a result of the ecology of agents and resources (i.e., from interactions between agents and resources, and between agents). This can lead to the appearance of seemingly paradoxical adaptation phenomena. For example, in an economy in which many firms compete, and where there are increasing returns to scale, it would be expected that there would be a trend toward a larger average firm size due to a growing concentration and centralization of activities. This would likely lead to firms having a more complex and rigid internal organization, but at the same time would give them a competitive advantage over smaller companies due to their higher productivity made possible by the increasing returns to scale. However, if uncertainty increases significantly due to rapid changes in consumer tastes, or due to a technological revolution that rapidly increases the rate of technological innovation in products and processes, smaller but more flexible companies are likely to have a competitive advantage over larger ones. So, we would see a decrease in the average size of companies, as the small ones would become the fittest.

6.3 Evolution and Economics

In the previous sections, we introduced the issue of evolution from artificial models such as genetic algorithms and artificial markets. But the discipline that deals with real evolutionary dynamics, and from which the contemporary concept of evolution originated, is the science of evolution, which is part of biology. So, it is appropriate to examine the way in which the concept of evolution is understood in that science, and then see the attempts made to extend its scope to the realm of economics.

The science of evolution teaches us that genetics and natural selection are very powerful concepts for explaining biological phenomena, and to some extent psychological and societal ones. As it is well known, the starting point of modern science of evolution are genes, those parts of genetic material arranged in a fixed order within a chromosome, that determine the features and the hereditary traits in living beings.

As emphasized by Richard Dawkins (2006), the primary goal of each gene is to "selfishly seek" its own replication indefinitely, within an environmental context of natural selection characterized by competition for scarce resources and the survival of the fittest. This leads each gene to establish relationships of conflict and cooperation with other genes. To formally capture the dynamics of these relationships, modern biology uses game theory tools. Indeed, it is from the replicating and "selfish" dynamics of each gene, within complex games of conflict/cooperation with other genes, that modern biology explains the existence, structure and functions of cells, tissues, organs, bodies, and species.[4]

Genes' behavior also explains – as emphasized by researchers such as Steven Pinker (2002) – the existence, form, and function of the most basic brain and mental structures in human beings, such as the capacity for reasoning and language, and the existence of emotions and capacities for socialization (such as the ability to put themselves in the place of the other), which are the result of the processes of evolutionary adaptation of the human species. In other words, the genetic/evolutionary logic determines, albeit in a very complex way, not only the basic programs or structures of living beings, but also some basic aspects of the human psyche.[5] Moreover, although very indirectly, it would also determine some of the universal structures that, it is claimed by some researchers such as Edward Wilson (1975 and 1978), underly the multiple forms of human societies.

However, we should note that, in the case of humans, culture is part of the environment or niche within which its genetic evolution occurred, so there has been a significant interaction between biology and culture that allows us to talk about genetic/cultural evolution, a field of research in which researchers such as Luigi Luca Cavalli-Sforza, Marcus Feldman, Robert Boyd, Peter Richerson, F. John Odling-Smee, and Kevin Laland stand out. This evolution operated not only in very long periods, but also in some instances in relatively short periods of a few thousand years, as, for example, in the case of the lactose tolerance gene, and as evidenced by other changes in the human genome over the last ten thousand years.

Evolutionary theory and methodology have transcended, almost since their inception, the realm of biology, and have been applied in economic, social, and even philosophical fields. In economics, the application of evolutionary concepts is long-standing. Thorstein Veblen, founding father of the school of economic thought known as institutionalism, was one of the pioneers in proposing, at the beginning of the twentieth century, that Darwinist concepts of variation, inheritance, and selection could be

---

[4] It should be noted that, even if the dynamics of each gene is "selfish" in the sense that it only "seeks" its replication, this does not prevent it from giving rise to phenotypes (set of observable characters in a living being that result from the interaction between its genotype and the medium in which it lives) that behave in a cooperative and altruistic manner, as a way of increasing its chances of replication.

[5] We should note that the genetic and adaptive determination of brain and mental functions and structures, although in some cases it is evident and relatively easy to find, in others it operates very indirectly and complexly, if at all. In general, today it is clear what happens when a gene is absent or neutralized, but not how the same gene operates its direct and, especially, its indirect effects when active.

applied to explain the evolution of socioeconomic institutions throughout history (Hodgson, 2004). At the same time, he maintained a critical perspective on ME in terms of the assumptions of fixed preferences and optimizing behavior.

Also, in the early twentieth century, Joseph Schumpeter developed an evolutionary vision of economic dynamic and coined the concept of "creative destruction," which refers to the introduction by entrepreneurs of waves of technological innovations at the process and product level, to replace the old products and processes. For Schumpeter, this is the essential feature of capitalism, which determines the long-term evolution of the economy, its fluctuations, and its processes of structural change. Schumpeter developed this concept in his famous 1911 work entitled, in German, *Theorie der wirtschaftlichen Entwicklung*, translated into English as *The Theory of Economic Development* (Schumpeter, 1983), although it should be noted that the German word *Entwicklung* may be translated as development or evolution. While Schumpeter's ideas were left aside for a long time, some of them returned reincarnated toward the end of the twentieth century in the work of neo-Schumpeterian economists such as Richard Nelson and Sidney Winter in the United States, and Giovanni Dosi in Europe.

The analysis of competition between firms from a Darwinist point of view was undertaken in a pioneering way in a work published by Armen Alchian (1950) who rationalized the workings of competitive markets as a process of survival of the fittest economic agents. While Alchian was a prominent ME figure, in that work he departs in some way from its basic assumptions, dismissing the explicit firm's maximization of an objective function (such as a profit function) as a fundamental rule of behavior. Since the future is uncertain due to imperfect anticipation and the intrinsic difficulty of humans to solve problems that involve many variables interacting in a complex way, Alchian argued that the success of a firm, that is, its survival in a competitive market, is the result of random decisions that are validated by the market situation in a given moment, rather than resulting from sophisticated rational plans. However, surviving firms, because they generate profits, will appear as if they have engaged in maximizing behavior. Other firms that imitate the behavior of surviving firms, will seem to be consciously deploying their own and optimal behavior, when in fact they are only copying the behavior of others. Thus, firms that survive the competitive process of "natural selection" will evolve by deploying behaviors that will indeed be optimal from the point of view of survival by profit maximization, while their goals and behavior may have been inspired by anything else. This would imply that, paradoxically, the assumption that economic agents act as if they maximize profit or utility rationally and optimally, even if they do not, is a useful device for analyzing the behavior of markets, a thesis also subscribed by Milton Friedman (1966) and Gary Becker (1962).

Nowadays, as we have seen in Chapter 2 in the Sugarscape model and in the evolutionary games of Chapters 3 and 7, artificial evolutionary processes are present in many AE models. In the Sugarscape, survival in the artificial evolutionary process depended on being able to meet a minimum level of metabolism, and the population evolved in such a way that survivors were those agents with lower metabolic needs and a higher range of vision. In the artificial evolutionary game of the prisoner's dilemma presented in Chapter 3, we simulated the process of evolution with genetic variation, inheritance, and selection, and observed how, in the long run, the surviving agents were only the defectors. In the artificial spatial evolutionary game of the prisoner's dilemma presented in Chapter 7, we simulate an evolutionary process in which each agent type is the result of its performance as compared to that of its neighbors. But these models do not exhaust the diversity of evolutionary AE models, as attested by many computationally implemented economic models that show evolutionary dynamics in processes of innovation and technological dissemination, in industrial competition, in finance, and in other areas of the economy.[6]

Although the application of the evolutionary methodology can illuminate some economic processes such as, for example, industrial competition, we must not lose sight of the fact that its indiscriminate application can lead us to the biologization of a discipline that, like economics, is eminently social. The main caveat to keep in mind when modeling economic processes from an evolutionary perspective, especially economy-wide institutional change and economic development, is that the indiscriminate biologization of social behaviors can lead us to see as natural and immutable, phenomena that originate historically in cultural and social practices. In this sense, it is convenient to consider the experiences of sociology and other social and human sciences, which generally take indiscriminate biological generalizations to the social realm with caution.

It should be remembered that social Darwinism (the vision of social transformation as a Darwinist process of natural selection) began to

---

[6] For a presentation of a variety of models of economic evolutionary dynamics, see, for example, Dawid and Pyka (2018).

develop after the mid-nineteenth century, especially in the work of evolutionist social theorists such as Herbert Spencer. For Spencer, analogous to biological phenomena, society evolves from undifferentiated to highly differentiated and functionally integrated forms. The forces of this evolution are, in his vision, population pressure and war, which determine evolutionary changes, especially in economic and political institutions. However, social Darwinism was set aside by the social sciences, especially from the second half of the twentieth century, due to its strong ideological uses (as an apology for wild capitalism, or as a Nazi apology of racial superiority) as well as because of what many considered as theoretical deficiencies, such as its teleological and progressive orientation that puts too much directionality to the historical flow; the use of a functionalist concept of adaptation; and the lack of a concept of agency, which for many social scientists is very relevant.[7] Evolutionism found its place today in the branch of sociology known as sociobiology, although it is far from being the main contemporary sociological theory.[8]

Even in the philosophical terrain, nowadays there are extensions of evolutionary theory that allows some thinkers to speak of universal or generalized Darwinism, as is the case of philosopher Daniel Dennett, who sees Darwinist evolution as a general algorithm of combination, mutation and selection/adaptation, which would prevail not only in biology, but would also apply to branches of science such as economics, psychology, linguistics, robotics, quantum physics, cosmology, and others (Dennett, 1996). This would transform generalized Darwinism into a theory with universal pretension, in the same vein as, for example, Ludwig von Bertalannfy's general theory of systems (von Bertalannfy, 2015), with which he tried to develop concepts and principles applicable to almost any field of knowledge. Universal transdisciplinary models are viewed with skepticism by canonical science.

---

[7] For a presentation of the pros and cons of evolutionism in the social sciences, see Sanderson (2006).

[8] In relation to sociobiology, it is worth noting its difference with biosociology. Sociobiology is a discipline that includes animal and human social phenomena within the neo-Darwinist evolutionary paradigm, while biosociology is oriented toward the study of the biological basis of human social behaviors or predispositions. While sociobiology emphasizes the role of genetic determinations in individual and social behavior, biosociology highlights the influence of social forms in people's evolutionary development, and even in their genome. For an introduction to biosociology, see Walsh (2014).

7

Artificial Complexity

The concept of complexity can be traced many centuries back in the history of thought and science. However, what is now known as the science of complexity emerged in recent decades from some branches of computer science, physics, chemistry, biology, and other related disciplines; took a major boost from the 1980s with the creation of the Santa Fe Institute (an interdisciplinary research center focused on the study of complex adaptive systems); and expanded recently into social sciences and economics, particularly within AE. Just like in the case of artificial evolutionary processes, the advancement in hardware and software technologies has made it possible for AE to simulate complex economic dynamics with powerful computational instruments.

A relatively simple way to get into the generation and illustration of complex artificial dynamics is through cellular automata. These have been one of the first computational instruments used to generate such dynamics. Originating in the 1940s with the work of Stanislaw Ulam and John von Neumann, its use for the study of complexity was specially developed by Stephen Wolfram from the 1980s.[1] In what follows we introduce the concept of cellular automaton and present one- and two-dimensional examples. Then we look at the basics of the science of complexity and discuss its applications in economics.[2]

---

[1] For a systematic introduction and presentation of cellular automata, see Wolfram (2002). For cellular automata theory and applications, see Li, Wu, and Li (2018). And for advanced methods of cellular automata analysis, see Hadeler and Müller (2017).

[2] Peter Albin was a pioneer in the application of cellular automata to economic problems. For a collection of his pathbreaking articles on the application of cellular automata and complexity theory in economics (edited and with a substantial introduction by Duncan Foley, another significant pioneer), see Albin (1998). For an illustrative example of an economic application of cellular automata, see Keenan and O'Brien (1993).

7.1 Cellular Automata

A cellular automaton is a model of a dynamic system that evolves in discrete steps. It is represented by a grid made up of cells, each of which can take a finite number of states. Cellular automata can be one-dimensional (a line of cells), two-dimensional (a cell plane), or have a larger number of dimensions. In what follows we will present one- and two-dimensional cellular automata.

7.1.1 A One-Dimensional Cellular Automaton

Figure 7.1 shows a cellular automaton made of a twenty-one-cell grid, which can take one of two states (black or white), with the central cell in the black state and all the others in white.

Each cell has a neighborhood of adjacent cells. In the Figure 7.1, for example, the central cell, which counting from left to right on the grid is cell number 11, has a neighborhood of two white cells, one to its left and one to its right. Cell 10's neighborhood is made up of cell 9, which is in a white state, and cell 11, which is in a black state. Etc.[3]

To generate the dynamic evolution of a cellular automaton, an initial state is defined by assigning each cell a state. A new generation of cells is obtained by applying a rule that defines the new state of each cell, depending on its present state and the states of each cell belonging to its neighborhood. This process is repeated iteratively.

Suppose that, as in our example, we have a one-dimensional cellular automaton made of a horizontal line of cells, and that each can be in one of two states, represented respectively by the color white or black. Let's define the following rule: each cell will be in the black state if it or any of the immediately adjacent ones were black in the previous generation (or step).

Visually, this rule can be represented as in Figure 7.2, where on the top line we have the previous state of the cell and its neighborhood, and in the lower line the corresponding new state of the cell (in the classification of

Figure 7.1 A one-dimensional cellular automaton with 21 cells

---

[3] Although here we represent the cellular automata as if it were a flat surface, actually it is a circular surface (a ring), that is, its ends are adjacent. Therefore, the neighborhood of cell number one is made up of cells 2 and 21, while that of cell 21 is made up of cells 20 and 1.

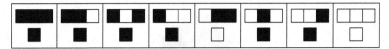

Figure 7.2 Wolfram rule number 254

cellular automata rules made by Wolfram, this rule is known as number 254).[4]

We can see that the representation captures the rule. The first element tells us that if a cell and its two neighbors are in a black state, that cell will remain in the black state. The second, that if a cell is in a black state, its left neighbor is in a black state, and its right neighbor in the white state, that cell will remain in the black state. Etc.

If we start from a forty-one-cell one-dimensional cellular automaton with an initial state in which all cells are white, except the middle cell that is black, and iterate the rule twenty times, we get a regular and predictable behavior, as can be seen in Figure 7.3, which shows us the evolution of our cellular automaton.

Now let's explore a new rule (rule number 90 in Wolfram's nomenclature), which states that a cell will be black whenever one or the other of its neighbors, but not both, has been black in the previous generation. The visual representation of this rule is shown in Figure 7.4.

Figure 7.5 shows the result of fifty iterations of a 101-cell cellular automaton following rule number 90, from an initial state analogous to the one in the previous example. We observe a pattern of nested structures that repeat in a similar way regardless of the scale. This type of figure is known as fractal, in this case a simple one. While the pattern is no longer as straightforward as in the previous example, it is regular and predictable.

---

[4] Wolfram's method of associating a number with each rule is as follows. If we assign the value one to the black state, and zero to the white state, from Figure 7.2 in the main text which graphically represents the rule we get, equivalently:

1	1	1	1	1	0	1	0	1	1	0	0	0	1	1	0	1	0	0	0	1	0	0	0
1			1			1			1			1			1			1			0		

The bottom row is the binary representation of the rule. The number 11111110 is an eight-digit binary number. To transform it into a decimal number we multiply each bit by the corresponding power of the number two, and thus we get the number 254:

$$1 \times 2^7 + 1 \times 2^6 + 1 \times 2^5 + 1 \times 2^4 + 1 \times 2^3 + 1 \times 2^2 + 1 \times 2^1 + 0 \times 2^0$$
$$= 1 \times 128 + 1 \times 64 + 1 \times 32 + 1 \times 16 + 1 \times 8 + 1 \times 4 + 1 \times 2 + 0 \times 1$$
$$= 254$$

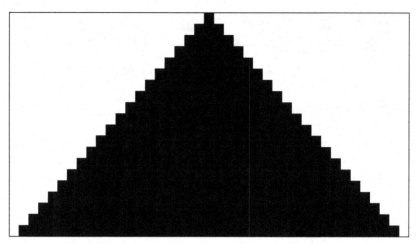

Figure 7.3 A 41-cell cellular automaton following Wolfram rule number 254 for 20 iterations

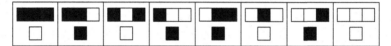

Figure 7.4 Wolfram rule number 90

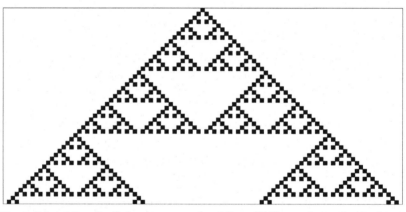

Figure 7.5 A 101-cell cellular automaton that follows Wolfram rule number 90 for 50 iterations

Let's finally explore a new rule (bearing the number 110) whose visual representation is in Figure 7.6.

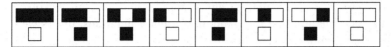

Figure 7.6 Wolfram rule number 110

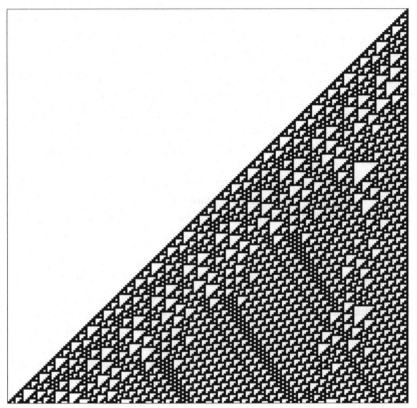

Figure 7.7 A 200-cell cellular automaton following Wolfram rule number 110 for 200 iterations

The result of 200 iterations of a 200-cell cellular automaton following rule number 110 from an initial state in which all cells are white, except the rightmost cell that is black, is shown in Figure 7.7.

We see that the dynamic does not seem either regular or random. In the evolution of this cellular automaton local structures emerge, are maintained for a while, and then change. This is an example of what is considered a complex dynamic. We have no way of predicting what would happen to the dynamic of this cellular automaton if we made it evolve by a thousand, one hundred thousand, or a million iterations, unless we perform that number of iterations.

Stephen Wolfram built a classification into classes of cellular automata rules, in which the state of each cell, as we have seen in the sample rules presented, depends on its state and that of its immediate left and right neighbors, in the previous generation. Given this structure, there are 256 possible rules and, according to the degree of complexity they generate, Wolfram grouped them into four classes:

Class 1: almost any initial state evolves rapidly into a homogeneous and stable state, and any initial randomness disappears.

Class 2: almost any initial state evolves rapidly into stable or oscillating structures, and if there is any initial randomness some of it will tend to remain, and local changes in the initial state will tend to remain localized.

Class 3: almost any initial state evolves chaotically, and local changes in the initial state tend to expand indefinitely.

Class 4: almost any initial state evolves in a complex way, with the formation of local structures that survive for long periods.

We might think that a structure of rules not as simple as those studied by Wolfram would generate a universe of behaviors even more diverse or complex. However, this is not necessarily the case: for example, it has been shown that rule number 110, which we saw and which belongs to class four, is what is known as Turing complete or universal. Colloquially speaking, this means that in principle a cellular automaton that followed this rule would be, in terms of the ability to generate simulations of dynamic processes, analogous to any real-world computer or supercomputer, no matter how complicated the programs that run on them.[5]

7.1.2 A Two-Dimensional Cellular Automaton

In Chapter 3, we introduced an evolutionary game based on the prisoner's dilemma. Here we will introduce a similar game, but with a spatial

---

[5] This is because several different systems of computation, such as cellular automata, Turing machines, sequential substitution systems (mappings that use a set of rules to transform elements of a sequence into a new sequence), and register machines (abstract machines similar to Turing machines that, instead of a head and tape, use multiple registers each holding a single positive integer), can emulate each other (i.e., in a way, they are fundamentally equivalent).

dimension, in the way Martin Nowak and Robert May did in their pioneering work (Nowak and May, 1992 and 1993). As in the Sugarscape model presented in Chapter 2, in this game players (agents) are on a two-dimensional grid of cells, but in this case all cells are occupied. Therefore, players do not move, but each remain in their cell, and the grid changes according to the changes that players experience as a function of their relationships with their neighbors. Thus, we're dealing with a two-dimensional cellular automaton.

In this artificial prisoner's dilemma spatial evolutionary game each player has a chromosome with only one gene, which can be equal to D (defect) or C (cooperate), and plays the prisoner's dilemma with all its immediate neighbors, and against itself. Figure 7.8 shows a player (black cell) and its eight immediate neighbors (white cells).

In the next round of games, the player adopts the strategy that got the highest accumulated payoff (the sum of the payoffs earned in all the games played) in the previous period. Such a strategy may be that of one of its neighbors, or its own. Note that in this game we do not assume either crossover or random mutation of chromosomes, but that the next generation inherits its gene (action) from the previous generation, according to the procedure just described.

Depending on the structure of payoffs, different dynamics are generated in this game. Particularly interesting is the one that results from a payoff matrix like the one shown in Figure 7.9, in which the dynamics critically depend on the numerical value of the b parameter.

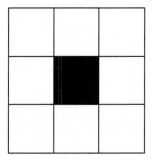

Figure 7.8 A player (black cell) and its neighborhood (white cells)

	Player 1	
	D	C

Player 2	D	0	0	b	0
	C	0	b	1	1

Figure 7.9 Payoff matrix of the artificial spatial evolutionary prisoner's dilemma game with two players

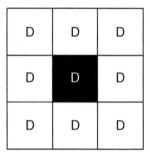

Figure 7.10 A defector in a neighborhood of defectors

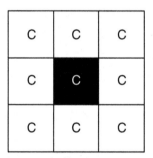

Figure 7.11 A cooperator in a neighborhood of cooperators

Let's see what happens when we have a defector, surrounded by a neighborhood of defectors, as shown in Figure 7.10.

According to the values in the payoff matrix, when the defector plays against itself it will get a payoff equal to zero, and the same will happen in each game against each of its neighbors. Its accumulated payoff will then be equal to zero. Now let's examine the case of a cooperator surrounded by cooperators, as shown in Figure 7.11.

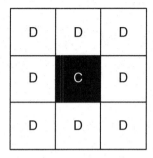

Figure 7.12 A cooperator in a neighborhood of defectors

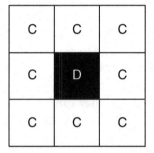

Figure 7.13 A defector in a neighborhood of cooperators

In this case, the payoff earned by the player in each game will be equal to one, and the accumulated payoff will be equal to nine. Now let's look at what happens when a cooperator, as shown in Figure 7.12, is surrounded by defectors.

In this case, the cooperator's payoff for playing against itself will be equal to one, while playing against a defector yields a payoff equal to zero. Thus, its accumulated payoff will be equal to one. Now let's see what happens when a defector is surrounded, as shown in Figure 7.13, by cooperators.

The payoff of playing against itself will be equal to zero, while the payoff of playing against a cooperator will be equal to b. Thus, its accumulated payoff will be equal to 8 × b. We see then that in this case the result each game against its neighbors, and the value of the accumulated payoff, will depend critically on the numerical value we give to b. For example, if b = 1, the accumulated payoff will be equal to eight (zero for playing against itself and eight times one for playing against each of its eight neighbors). This result is lower than that obtained by a cooperator surrounded by cooperators, as we saw in the corresponding example and that was equal to nine.

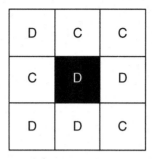

Figure 7.14 A defector in a diverse neighborhood

So, in a neighborhood of cooperators, cooperation would tend to prevail as a playing strategy. However, if we set b = 2, the accumulated payoff for the defector will be equal to 16. Therefore, in a neighborhood of cooperators, the defector's strategy would tend to spread, as it would be adopted by all its neighbors as it had the highest payoff.

Of course, not all neighborhoods will necessarily be as homogeneous as the ones we've considered, but they can be made up of the most varied setups of cooperators and defectors, resulting in accumulated payoffs with values also very varied. In other words, we could have combinations like the one shown in Figure 7.14, and many others.

Trying to analyze all possible neighborhood configurations and the corresponding accumulated payoffs would be a very tedious job. Moreover, we should keep in mind that each of the players within a neighborhood has in turn its own neighborhood, and that the issue becomes more complex as the size of the two-dimensional grid of cells in which the players are located becomes larger, as the number of neighborhoods grows rapidly. This forces us to attack the problem through computer simulations.[6]

Figure 7.15 shows the evolution of the game in a grid of 15 × 15 cells (i.e., in total there are 325 agents, each playing against its neighbors and against itself) and in nine periods, and where parameter b = 6. Each cell is colored as the agent's behavior has been in the immediately preceding period, compared to his behavior in the current period, according to the following rule: if it was defector and remains a defector, the color is black; if it went

---

[6] The two-dimensional grids used in the simulations, as it was also the case in the Sugarscape model grid presented in Chapter 2, are represented in the text as a square and flat surface. However, actually they are the surface of a Torus (a geometrical object that has the shape of a donut). Therefore, the cells at their upper and lower ends, and at their left and right ends, are adjacent.

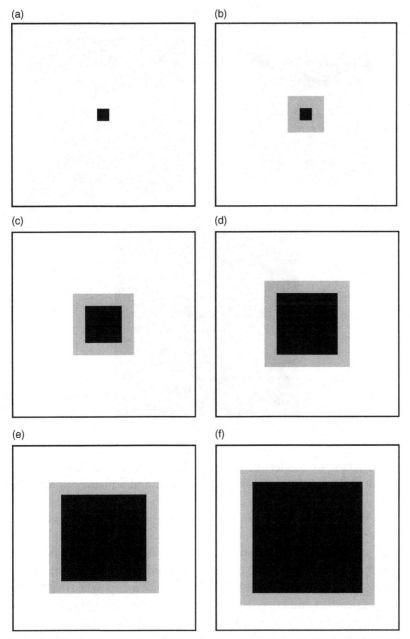

Figure 7.15 Evolution of the population of agents along nine periods (from left to right and from top to bottom), with parameter b = 6

(g)   (h)

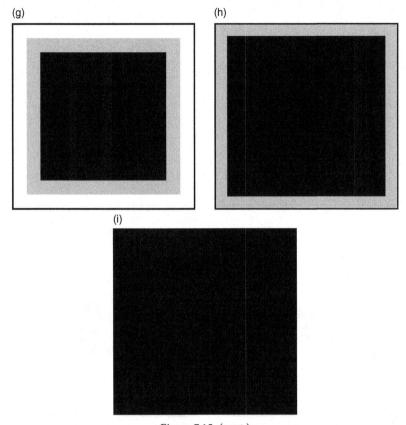

(i)

Figure 7.15 (cont.)

from defector to cooperator, dark gray; if it went from cooperator to defector, light gray; and if it was a cooperator and remains a cooperator, white.

The simulation begins in an initial period (panel a) in which all agents are cooperators (white color), except one located in the center of the grid (black color), which is a defector. We can see that the population of defectors progressively expands. In the second period (panel b), we see that the defector is surrounded by light-gray-colored players, that is, they were cooperators and are now defectors. In the third period (panel c), the population of defectors expanded (there are several black cells) and in turn there are more cooperators who became defectors, which is evident in a larger light-gray box than in the previous period. The process is repeated each period, until finally all the cooperators have mutated their cooperator gene by a defector gene (panel i). And we can attribute this to the relatively high value of the b parameter, which is a strong incentive to defect.

Figure 7.16 shows the results of a simulation of the game on a grid of 69 × 69 cells (i.e., in total there are 4,761 players, each playing against its neighbors and against itself) and fifty-five periods, and where parameter b = 1.85. The cells are colored according to the same criterion as in the previous simulation. Similarly, the simulation begins in an initial period (panel a) in which all agents are cooperators (white color), except one located in the center of the grid (black color), which is a defector. From left to right, and from top to bottom, we see the evolution of the population of players, every five periods, until period fifty-five.

The dynamic evolution of this simulation shows us a situation in which defectors expand for several periods, but then the cooperators gain ground again, without a clear predominance of one or the other. We can also observe a particularly interesting behavior. The evolutionary dynamic of the game does not seem completely random or completely predictable: it displays an "evolutionary kaleidoscope" in which structures appear and remain approximately the same for some time, are then replaced by different structures that also show some persistence, and so on.

7.2 Complexity and Economics

In the previous sections, we introduced the issue of complexity from relatively simple artificial systems such as cellular automata. But there are multiple systems (biological, economic, social, etc.), in which dynamics are observed that could be described as complex, although it should be noted that the concept of a complex system, and therefore its definition, is a matter of controversy.

Let's begin by saying that complex systems are usually defined as those made of multiple elements interacting in nonlinear ways (i.e., some causes or disturbances may provoke nonproportional effects) and with positive feedback (elements' behaviors can reinforce or amplify each other). These systems evolve over time, showing emergent properties, where emergence is understood as the development of a new characteristic, behavior, or structure, qualitatively different from that displayed by the system at a previous stage.[7]

---

[7] For a very accessible introduction to the science of complexity, see Mitchell (2009). For a more advanced introduction, see Miller and Page (2007). For an advanced presentation of how models of complex systems are built, and of the mathematical tools used for studying their dynamics, see Boccara (2004).

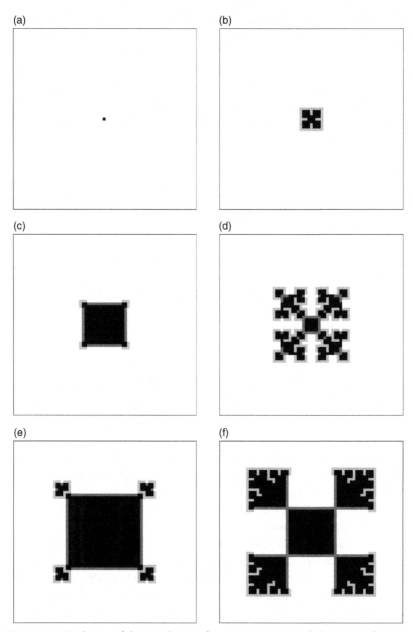

Figure 7.16 Evolution of the population of agents over 55 periods (one every five periods shown, from left to right, and from top to bottom), with parameter b = 1.85

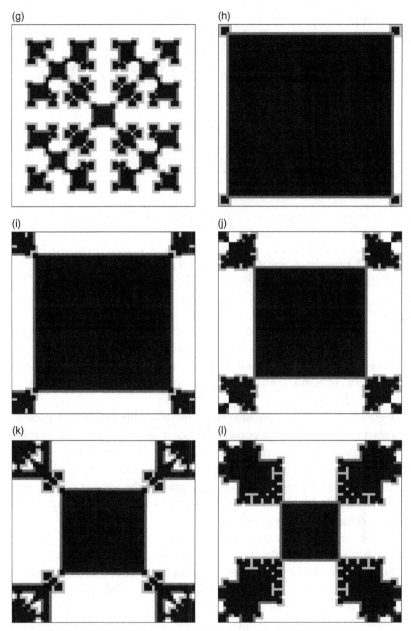

Figure 7.16 (cont.)

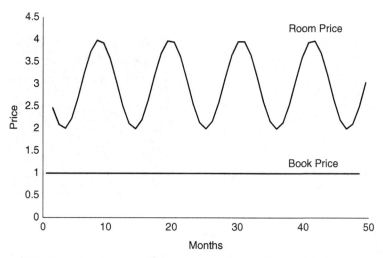

Figure 7.17 Examples of constant dynamic (book price) and cyclical dynamic (price of a hotel room that changes regularly according to the season)

One classification that helps to delimit the definition of a complex system is the following. First, there are very simple ordered systems that are in equilibrium: left to themselves, they remain indefinitely in the same state or in a cycle, unless an external cause or disturbance takes them out of it.

Figure 7.17 shows two possible examples of equilibrium, both representing the price evolution of a good or service over time. In the first example (the horizontal line) the price remains constant for a long time, as might be the case of the price of a book. The second example shows regular cyclic fluctuations due to seasonal phenomena, such as the price of a hotel room that increases in high season and decreases in low season. In both cases, future evolution is easily predictable.

Second, there are very active or disordered systems, which are always in disequilibrium and display random behavior. Figure 7.18 shows an example, which could be the daily evolution of the price of a stock in the stock market. In this example, future evolution is impossible to predict, even from one day to the next.

Third, we have complex systems that are between the two extreme cases that we presented previously: they can exhibit a behavior for a while, and then suffer important discontinuities, with self-reorganizations that lead to structural changes and a new behavior, and so on, thus deploying a

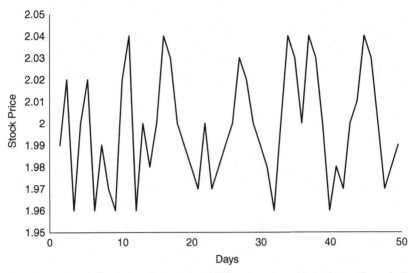

Figure 7.18 Example of a random process (daily price of a stock in the stock market)

complex dynamic.[8] Figure 7.19 shows an example, which could be interpreted as the historical evolution of a country's standard of living over decades, or even centuries. At first the country has a very backward and rudimentary fishing economy with a constant standard of living. It then moves to an agrarian economy system based on fruit production with strong seasonality, leading to a regularly fluctuating standard of living. Then the country industrializes, and its standard of living grows systematically. But from some point on, the ecological deterioration caused by uncontrolled industrialization leads to a climate disaster that results in the systematic deterioration of living standards. We see that the evolution of this system, while predictable within certain periods, is not predictable as we increase the temporal range of observation. In this hypothetical example, we cannot know how long the decline in living standards will continue, whether the country will undergo a reversal to an agricultural or fishing economy, whether it will return to the path of industrial development, or whether it will have another type of economy that we can't even imagine.

---

[8] Sometimes the notion of "edge of chaos" is used to refer to complex systems, meaning that these systems are in a region between order and chaos or full randomness. However, it should be noted that it is a notion that is not rigorously defined.

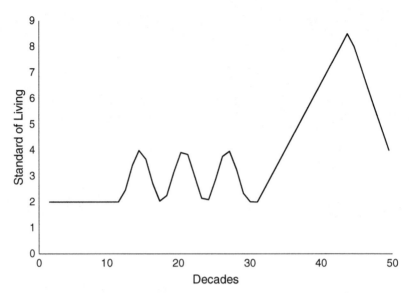

Figure 7.19 Example of complex dynamic (historical evolution a country's standard of living over 50 decades)

Another way to define a complex system is based on the concepts of feedback and emergence. In noncomplex systems, behaviors of various types cancel each other (negative feedback) as the size of the system grows, resulting in a stable and predictable average behavior. For example, a price increase decreases the demand for a good, while a price decrease increases demand. And the more people who participate in the market for that good, the more likely deviations from the equilibrium price will cancel each other: if there are people who are willing to pay more than the equilibrium price, this will be compensated by the existence of people willing to pay less.[9]

In complex systems, the behaviors of agents are sometimes reinforced by each other due to coupling or positive feedback, and they cause the emergence of complex aggregate behaviors, sometimes in the form of critical or catastrophic changes. For example, so-called self-fulfilling prophecies illustrate a case of positive feedback between expectations and behaviors. If market participants expect a continuous rise in the price of a good, they will try to purchase that good, significantly increasing demand

---

[9] This type of behavior is at the basis of the applicability of the law of large numbers, the central limit theorem, and normal probability distributions, to a multitude of phenomena.

and thus causing a price rise. In this way, their expectations of a raising price will be validated, which will lead them to further increase demand, causing another price rise, and so on. Another example is a bank run. A rumor of a bank's possible bankruptcy may lead to a massive withdrawal of deposits, effectively causing its bankruptcy. This would raise doubts as to the solvency of other banks and would therefore lead to the withdrawal of deposits and subsequent bankruptcy, and so on putting the entire banking system at risk.[10]

Finally, as another definitional characteristic of a complex system, it is often emphasized that the only way to know the future evolution of a complex system is through its computational simulation during as many periods as necessary, since there is no way of knowing a priori what this evolution will be, that is, of predicting it before simulating it.

At this point, we can raise the following question: Is there a general model of complex systems? So far there isn't, since the very definition of complex system is discussed. Is there an objective and universal metric of complex systems? Not at the moment, for the notion of complexity would seem to have a strong subjective burden.[11] Indeed, a dynamic process may seem simple for a while, complex if you observe it for longer, simple if you look at it even more, and even within the same period it may seem simple to one observer and complex to another.

Are there any specific objective measures of complexity? In fact, there are several, most of which come from computer science and information theory. Within them, the measure developed within what is known as algorithmic theory of information in the 1960s – with contributions from physicist Ray Solomonoff, and mathematicians Andrey Kolmogorov and Gregory Chaitin – stands out. This is a measure of complexity applicable to data structures, such as a sequence of numbers or characters. The measure of the degree of complexity of these structures is given by the shorter length of the algorithm (or, equivalently, the computer program) that can generate such a structure as a result of its execution. For example, a sequence of numbers like the following:

0123456789

can be generated by a very short algorithm, such as the following:

---

[10] Unlike the phenomena of negative feedback, from a statistical point of view the phenomena of positive feedback are captured better with power laws and probability distributions with heavy tails.

[11] For a presentation and discussion of the definitions and measures of complexity, see Standish (2008), and Mitchell (2009), pp. 94–111.

Step 1: Print the number 0.
Step 2: Add 1 to the last printed number.
Step 3: Print the obtained number.
Step 4: If the number obtained is greater than 9, end the program, otherwise go back to step 2.

But a sequence like the following:

9327650148

could not be generated more than by repeating the whole sequence with a ten-step program like the following:

Step 1: Print the number 0.
Step 2: Print the number 1.

...

Step 9: Print the number 8.
Step 10: Print the number 9 and end the program.

The aforementioned example is very rudimentary, and we present it only for the purpose of providing an intuition of what is meant by measure of algorithmic complexity. But such a measure can be applied to much larger and more diverse data structures and algorithms. The example also serves to illustrate a peculiar feature of the measure of algorithmic complexity. The first sequence of numbers we were able to generate with a short program because it obeys a law: each number is the result of adding one unit to the next. With this knowledge, we would be able to generate a sequence of ten, one thousand, one million, or billions of numbers, without adding steps to our program, that is, without increasing its complexity. The second sequence of numbers does not obey any law – it is completely random, and therefore we cannot "compress" it into a shorter program than the sequence itself. It follows that, from the point of view of algorithmic complexity, something is more complex the more random (i.e., the less "compressible" in an algorithm) it is. This measure seems to clash conceptually with the intuitive concept of a complex system. For example, an irrational number containing infinite decimal places and whose sequence has no regularity – that is, that it lacks structure – would be more complex than an artificial economic system whose structure can be represented and simulated with a computer program that has a finite number of instructions.

When we previously introduced a definition of a complex system, we mentioned that one of its characteristics was emergence. For what is known as emergentism, the interaction of a set of elements at a lower level can result in the emergence, at a higher level, of a new type of entity or structure, qualitatively different, which in turn can restrict or condition the lower level. For example, from the chemical interaction of molecules living beings emerge, which would not be reducible to pure chemistry; from the interaction of neurons the mind emerges, which would not be reducible to the mere brain; from the interaction of individuals social structures emerge, which would not be reducible to an individual level. On the other hand, for what is known as reductionism, what seem to be emergent phenomena are reducible to the interactions of lower-level elements.

Emergentism has a long tradition, usually based on the use of expressive metaphors, but is viewed with skepticism by scientific orthodoxy, more akin to reductionist postures. Nevertheless, in recent decades emergentism has acquired more respectability with the development of the science of complexity.[12]

Is there an objective measure applicable to emergent phenomena? Just as there is no universal objective measure of complexity, there is also no such measure of emergent phenomena. The problem here is how to quantify and compare what is qualitatively different, since what for one observer can be substantially different, for another may not be. There is no universal measure of emergence, but again, it is within the field of computer science and information theory where some specific measures have been developed. For example, James Crutchfield proposes a measure in which emergent levels differ according to the power of the information processing architecture necessary to describe each of them.[13]

Finally, we can ask ourselves one last question: Can the adoption of methods and models of the science of complexity contribute significantly to the advancement of economics?

---

[12] For an introductory discussion of emergentism, see Pigliucci (2004). For a defense of emergentism, see physics Nobel Prize winner Phillip Anderson (1972). For a defense of reductionism, see physics Nobel Prize winner Stephen Weinberg (1993).

[13] The measure proposed by James Crutchfield (1994) is based on a hierarchy of automata classes (these automata are different from the cellular automata we saw in this chapter: they are computational models that, from an initial state, apply a transition function and move from one state to another until they reach a final state). Each class of automata is attributed an information processing structure: logical operations, memory, and information transmission. A system experiences emergence if at one point the information processing architecture changes in such a way that a different and more powerful level of intrinsic computation appears, and was not present in the previous conditions. That is, when we need an automaton of a higher class to describe the new state of the system. For other measures of emergence, see Gershenson and Fernández (2012).

The social sciences have, from time to time, adopted novel methods and models from mathematics and related disciplines. In the second half of the twentieth century, the application to the study of society of concepts and methods of cybernetics (the scientific study and modeling of processes of control and communication in animals and machines) and systems theory (the general modeling of systems' dynamics) gained momentum in the hands of functionalist/systemic sociological theorists such as Talcott Parsons and Niklas Luhmann.

For Parsons and Luhmann society was a multilevel system subject to differentiation and vertical and horizontal integration, with an inherent tendency toward equilibrium instrumented by negative feedback, a typical concept from cybernetics, and by homeostasis, a typical concept from systems theory, two disciplines that took their first steps in those times. It was precisely the emphasis on this concept of social equilibrium, later seen as a conservative and reactionary, that led to the decadence of such theories from the 1960s, when the explanation of, and push for, social change in a world that mutated rapidly and broke with many traditional social and cultural rules, became of the utmost relevance (Bailey, 2006). Today, the science of complexity is being incorporated into some branches of the social sciences, but emphasizing, instead of the concept of equilibrium typical of the functionalist/systemic approach to social science, the concepts of permanent disequilibrium and transformation, that is, positive over negative feedback (Carley, 2006).

In the field of economics there are also developments that incorporate elements of the science of complexity, especially within AE. We should warn that, although many see the analysis of complex systems as an essential and defining feature of AE, that is not necessarily the case. There are AE models that display noncomplex evolutionary dynamics, as we saw in Chapter 2 in the Sugarscape model with trade, that converged toward a situation of equilibrium in population and prices, albeit of a statistical nature. We also saw this in Chapter 3 with the evolutionary prisoner's dilemma game that converged toward a Nash equilibrium. But there are models of artificial markets and evolutionary games that neither seem to converge toward equilibrium nor to be completely random, as is the case of the evolutionary spatial game we presented in the form of a two-dimensional cellular automata. And there are other cases of evolutionary games (e.g., games that implement learning strategies with prizes and punishments, or in which a player misunderstands what the opponent did in the previous move, or in which a player does not implement the choice she thought, or other sophistications in the modeling of players' strategies) which may generate complex dynamics (Albin, 1992; Axelrod, 1997).

There are also many other AE models from which complex dynamics emerge. For example, within the field of finance, we can mention the famous artificial stock market model developed at the Santa Fe Institute. Prominent economists such as W. Brian Arthur and Blake LeBaron, along with computer scientist John Holland (the founding father of the field of genetic algorithms), physicist Richard Palmer, and computer scientist Paul Taylor worked on this model, one of the pioneering attempts to develop a model of a financial market with heterogeneous agents and learning. Originally, the main goal was to model and test a stock market populated with heterogeneous and boundedly rational learning agents, instead of the fully rational agents common in equilibrium modeling in ME. The model showed that, depending on the value of a parameter characterizing the learning speed of agents, its behavior may converge to a regime close to a rational expectations equilibrium,[14] or not converge and display complex dynamics. Over time, different refinements were introduced to the model (LeBaron, 2002; Ehrentreich, 2008).

As we mentioned before, a definitional characteristic of a complex system is its strong unpredictability. It is worth mentioning that this unpredictability poses a challenge to economic planning and to the conventional way of doing economic policy modeling, which usually consists of performing counterfactual policy analysis (using discretionary or rule-based policies) with mathematical or econometric models displaying a deterministic or stochastic but somehow predictable behavior. This challenge was already present, in some way, in the debate that took place in the 1920s and 1930s and that had as main protagonists Ludwig von Mises and Friedrich Hayek on the one hand, and Oskar Lange and Abba Lerner on the other, and that it is known as the economic calculation debate. Hayek (1937 and 1945) and the Austrian school of economics emphasized that the market and the price system are a complex mechanism of self-organization from which a spontaneous order emerges, a mechanism that cannot be substituted by a central planning mechanism due to its inherent complexity; Lange and Lerner claimed that there is an equivalence between a

---

[14] When rational expectations, also known as model-consistent expectations, are assumed in a stochastic model of the economy, that means that the agents in the model are assumed to know the model and that, on average, they take the model's predictions as true. Therefore, a rational expectations equilibrium is an economic equilibrium in which agents' expectations with respect to the evolution of the economic variables generated by the model coincide with the actual evolution of those model variables.

centrally planned system of the economy and an economic system of perfect competition. The way of conceiving the complexity of the economic system by Hayek and the Austrian school, although less formal and mathematized, is a strong antecedent of the way it is conceived today in the field of complexity economics, which uses the concepts and the formal and computational tools of the contemporaneous science of complexity (Rosser, 2015). Furthermore, some current proposals on the way of performing policymaking when facing complexity explicitly acknowledge their link with Hayek's thinking, and advocate a softer "bottom-up" way of policymaking instead of the stronger conventional "top-down" view and procedures. This is somewhat surprising, since much of complexity economics was developed as a critique of ME, which views the market as a mechanism that always tends toward equilibrium, and state intervention as counterproductive.[15]

Anyway, there are still doubts as to whether the incorporation of elements of the science of complexity into economics will constitute a genuine advance or just one more fashion, becoming something like the fourth event in the sequence of the so-called "Four Cs": cybernetics, catastrophes, chaos, and complexity. Cybernetics had its beginnings in the 1940s from the works of mathematician Norbert Wiener and as we mentioned earlier influenced the works of Parsons and Luhmann. Catastrophe theory (a mathematical theory that models sudden and discontinuous transitions between the states of a system, given smooth variation of the underlying parameters) was introduced by mathematician René Thom in the late 1950s and had some influence on the social sciences in the late 1960s and during the 1970s. Chaos theory (a branch of mathematics that studies nonlinear systems that are very sensitive to changes in initial conditions) has a long trajectory in the history of mathematics, but was influential in social sciences from the 1980s mainly through to the joint work of chemistry Nobel Prize winner Ilya Prigogine and philosopher Isabelle Stengers. Similarly, while various lines of thought around complex systems can be traced back for long time, it could be said that what is now known as science of complexity makes its appearance with the founding of the Santa Fe Institute in 1984, the first research institution whose work was explicitly focused on the study of complex systems and which immediately included the work of social scientists.[16]

---

[15] For contemporary presentations of the softer "bottom-up" way of performing policymaking when facing complexity, see Brock and Colander (2000) and Colander and Kupers (2014). For a critical appraisal, see Velupillai (2005).

[16] For a presentation of the characteristics, history, and research projects of the Santa Fe Institute, see the website www.santafe.edu.

For some critics, such as John Horgan (1995 and 2015), the concepts and methods of these disciplines (the "Four Cs") would have been a succession of interdisciplinary fads that promised more than they delivered in terms of new knowledge, although we can also find much more optimistic visions. Within the field of economics, two decades ago, J. Barkley Rosser Jr. (1999) argued that some common perspective was being formed with the emergence of each of the Cs, and that it could be reaching a critical mass to further influence the thinking of economists. And more recently, we came across strong statements. Richard Holt, J. Barkley Rosser Jr., and David Colander (Holt, Rosser, and Colander, 2010) argue that the era of ME is finished and that it is being replaced by the age of complexity. Similarly, W. Brian Arthur (2014) states that the economics of complexity is a different way from that of ME to think about the economy; that ME is a particular case of complexity economics in that equilibrium-focused analysis is a particular case of disequilibrium analysis; and that the shift in economic analysis from ME toward complexity would reflect a more general shift at the science level – from a Newtonian approach and method, based on equations and continuity, to the algorithmic and procedural "Turingesc" approach and method. However, there are also intermediate positions, such as that of Steven Durlauf (2012), who argues that complexity can improve the essentially mathematical approach to economic analysis typical of ME, but in a complementary and nonsubstitute way.

From what we have seen so far, it would be premature to judge whether the incorporation of the concepts of the science of complexity into economics will bring significant advances. So, the answer to the above question remains open.

Artificial Economics and the Agent/Structure Problem

What is known as the agent/structure problem has been, and still is, a major issue of discussion within the social sciences. For individualist/reductionist positions, social phenomena we perceive as structural (social stratification, institutions, social networks, social norms) would be merely appearances to be explained through the behavior of individual actors. On the contrary, for structuralist/holistic positions, social phenomena can be explained by the operation of underlying social structures that severely constrain the behavior of individuals. In extreme versions of these positions, what we perceive as individual agents would be nothing more than appearances derived from the operation of those structures. Finally, there are intermediate positions that claim that agents and structures are dynamically generated from each other.

AE methodology offers an interesting way of approaching the agent/structure problem. We have seen that AE works with computational simulations of economic systems. Artificial agents are the basic units that make up such systems. They are computational objects inside of which there is information and rules of processing, and that interact with each other. Various structures emerge from the simulation of these interactions. In turn, these structures may cause changes in agents, affecting both their information sets and their behavioral rules. In this Chapter we present the main positions in economics and in the social sciences with respect to the agent/structure problem, and explore some contributions that can be made from AE.

8.1 Individualism, Structuralism, and Intermediate Postures

The goal of the social sciences is to understand the functioning of social systems. Correspondingly, the one of economics is to understand economic systems. A good starting point to introduce the various positions toward the agent/structure problem is to start from the definition of the system concept. A system is defined as a set of elements along with the set of relationships between them. The structure of the system is the set of these relationships, and their isomorphic transformations, that is, those that preserve the shape of the structure. For example, if we have an economic system made of two sectors – the agricultural and the industrial – the relative resizing of these sectors does not alter the economic structure. Different would be the case where a new sector, such as services, emerges, resulting in a new structure.

The individualist/reductionist stance within the social sciences emphasizes the role of individuals as the fundamental elements of social and economic systems. That is to say that it prioritizes the role of the elements of the system, and the degrees of freedom of their behavior, over the constraints emanating from their interrelationships. The individualist/reductionist position begins from the study of the behavior of individuals, which is modeled as a problem of optimization of well-being given a set of invariant preferences, subject to a resource constraint. Structural phenomena such as income distribution and social stratification are obtained as the aggregation of the results of the behaviors of individuals and are not recognized for an existence of their own or qualitatively different.

The origins of this approach can be traced back to the work of utilitarian thinkers such as Jeremy Bentham and John Stuart Mill, while early mathematical formulations are closely linked to the work of the pioneers of the marginalist revolution in economics in the late nineteenth century: William Stanley Jevons, Carl Menger, and Leon Walras. Contemporaneously, the individualist/reductionist stance is dominant within ME, and it appears within the social sciences in what is known as rational choice theory, which in some ways expresses the "imperialist expansion" of ME assumptions and methods toward other disciplines, as illustrated, for example, by Gary Becker's work (Becker, 1993).

The structuralist/holistic position prioritizes the role of structures (i.e., of the networks of interrelationships) over the individual elements of the economic system. Its starting point is the study of structural phenomena such as social stratification, interrelationships between economic sectors, income distribution, exchange networks, etc., while the degrees of freedom of behavior of individuals are strongly constrained by their position within the networks of interrelations in which they are immersed.

The origins of structuralism can be traced in the early twentieth century in the linguistic works of Ferdinand de Saussure, and later in the anthropological research of Claude Lévi-Strauss, and had a strong influence in the social sciences in the 1950s and 1960s, and then went down. In economics, structuralism is associated with the thinking of the pioneers of development economics, particularly with the work of the United Nations Economic Commission for Latin America from the 1950s. Structuralist economic thinking pointed to cross-sectoral relations as determinants of economic development, and it did so in two main ways (Chenery, 1975): by claiming that development takes place unequally between economic sectors (hypothesis formulated by Arthur Lewis and Raúl Prebisch); or by emphasizing the complementarities between sectors that determine the conditions for balanced growth of the economic system (hypothesis developed by Paul Rosestein-Rodan and Ragnar Nurkse).

Outside the field of development economics, there are important general models that can be qualified as structuralist. For example, Wassily Leontieff's (1941) famous input-output model is a representation of the structure of relationships between all sectors of an economy, in which outputs of one sector are inputs for other sectors and where cross-sectoral flows of goods and services are determined by structural relationships of a purely technical nature. Given a final demand vector, the model determines all quantities produced in the economy.

Piero Sraffa's production-prices model also captures multiple cross-sectoral relationships, along with a representation of two social classes (workers and capitalists) through their respective incomes: wages and the rate of profit. The title of the famous Sraffa's book, *Production of Commodities by Means of Commodities* (1960), gives us an indication that within his model there is no direct role for individual agents: there is a structure that, given the average rate of profit or, alternatively, the average wage, determines all the relative prices of the economy and reproduces itself.

As for intermediate positions, they try to articulate visions, narratives, and models, of social and economic systems in which the elements (i.e., individuals or agents) and their networks of interrelationships (structures) are generated by dialectical or circular causality processes.

The dialectical vision of the agent/structure or individual/society relationship has a long history that goes back to Marxist dialectic. Within this tradition the individual, the subject, is objectified in the outside world by giving a human form to it through its constituent practice of material and social structures. And in turn these structures, socially and historically built, are internalized by individuals in their practical lives and thus build their subjectivity. It is then in social practice that the dialectical unity between agent and structure become apparent (Lefevre, 2009).

Nowadays there are other influential intermediate positions, mainly from the field of sociology, among which are Pierre Bourdieu's theory of practice and Anthony Giddens's theory of structuration.

Bourdieu tries to capture the dialectics of the "externalization of internality and internalization of externality." To this end, he develops the concepts of *habitus* and field (Bourdieu, 1977). Habitus results from a set of historical relationships that are "deposited" in the bodies of individuals, in the form of bodily and mental schemes of perception, appreciation, and action (i.e., they are not formal or explicit rules of behavior). A field is a social space that is the result of a set of objective historical relationships. It displays games of permanent dispute over the control of capital, where capital is any resource that gives power and makes domination possible, and which can take various forms: economic, social, cultural, symbolic. The concepts of field and *habitus* reflect two modes of existence of the social: a field is the social transformed into a thing (something objective) and the *habitus* is the social inscribed in the body (something subjective). Social practices arise from the dialectical relationship between *habitus* and field. So, to understand the practices of individuals we need to understand their *habitus* and their position within the fields in which they act.

For Giddens, the concept of structure refers to the rules and resources that condition social life (Giddens, 1986). Structures exist in the form of agents' *memory traces* (i.e., they are immersed in the organic bases of human cognitive ability) and are instantiated through agents' actions. Therefore, structures exist internally (within agents as memory traces) and at the same time externally (as a result or manifestation of agents' social actions). They condition the actions of agents, but simultaneously are the historical result of their past actions. Thus, for Giddens, social life is a recursive process where structure is both the medium and the result of the reproduction of social practices. During social practice, agent and structure are constituted simultaneously.

Individualist/reductionist and structuralist/holistic approaches, especially in the field of economics, have reached a high degree of formal sophistication, usually through mathematical modeling. This is not the case of intermediate positions, some of which we have introduced previously. These are mostly developed in narrative arguments, sometimes not very rigorous[1]: in some cases, concepts and definitions are "piled up" one

---

[1] As a somewhat exceptional case, we can mention the work of Oskar Lange (Lange, 1965), who attempted to mathematically formalize the narrative of Marxist dialectic using concepts from cybernetics.

on top of the other.[2] As a way of making more precise or to complement narrative arguments, AE computational methods could contribute, as we will see in what follows, to explore the reciprocal generation between agents and structures.

8.2 Artificial Economics and Agent/Structure Feedback

As we have seen in previous chapters, AE generates economies from the local interaction of artificial agents. This could lead to inscribe AE, like ME, within the reductionist/individualist position. Even though, as we saw in Chapter 4, ME is a discipline that models economic phenomena mathematically, while AE generates them computationally.

Indeed, most AE models work in a one-way generation mode: the social (the macro) results from interactions between agents (the micro), but not the other way around (O'Sullivan and Haklay, 2000). Unlike ME, however, there is nothing in principle preventing AE's artificial agents (their databases and rules of conduct) from undergoing changes as a result of their economic interactions. Let's look at some examples based on artificial markets and artificial games models that we have introduced in previous chapters.

In Chapter 2, we presented an artificial economy model with movement and exchange. In this model, agents collected two resources (sugar and spice) and, according to their preferences and their stocks of each resource, exchanged them with their neighbors. Throughout the simulations, agent preferences did not change. The fixed preference assumption is a fundamental assumption of ME and the same applies in practically all its models. However, the flexibility of AE simulations allows us to lift this assumption and simulate a process of endogenous change of preferences derived from the economic interaction between agents.

For this we will introduce in the model of Chapter 2 a process of cultural evolution based on which the preferences of the agents will be determined, analogously to how Joshua Epstein and Robert Axtell (Epstein and Axtell, 1996) do in the Sugarscape model. There is a long tradition that models the processes of cultural evolution assuming that just as there are units of biological information in genes, there are units of cultural information called memes (a term created by Richard Dawkins) or cultural labels.[3] And

---

[2] For a critique of Giddens's theory of structuration in this regard, see Turner (1986). For a critique of Bourdieu's theory of practice, see Turner (1994).

[3] Dawkins introduced the concept and the word "meme" in 1976 in his famous book on the "selfish gene" (Dawkins, 2006). Pioneering systematic works in this line have been those of Cavalli-Sforza and Feldman (1981), and Boyd and Richerson (1985).

just as genes form a chromosome, cultural labels are similarly assumed to form cultural chains. Assume then that each agent in the Sugarscape model, in addition to having attributes such as range of vision, metabolism, and preferences, also has a cultural attribute, and that we encode that attribute with a chain of labels in which each label represents a cultural trait of the agent. For example, the label of the first position in the chain may correspond to its type of clothing, the second to the music it listens to, the third to the type of literature it reads, etc. Suppose there are two distinct cultures, the red (R) and the green (G), and that the tag string for an agent's cultural attribute contains twenty-one tags. So, a string like the following:

RRRRRRRRRRRRRRRRRRRRR

indicates that all the cultural features of the agent correspond to the red culture, while the string:

RRGGGRGRGGGGGRRRRRRGGG

indicates that the agent's cultural attribute is a mixture of the two cultures: it dresses as in the red culture, listens to the music of that culture, but reads the literature of the green culture, etc.

As we saw in the Sugarscape model with trade presented in Chapter 2, in this model, agents interact with their neighbors through the exchange of resources. We will now assume that cultural interaction also occurs in such interaction. For example, consider the following mechanism: when agent A and agent B meet to exchange resources, we randomly select one of the labels in agent B's chain and replace it with the corresponding label from agent A. That is, there is a process of cultural influence from agent A to B. Finally, we establish a criterion to determine when an agent belongs to the red cultural group and when to the green. Suppose that f is the fraction of tags equal to R in the agent tag string. The criterion is as follows: if more than half of the labels in an agent's cultural chain are red (i.e., if f is greater than 0.5) the agent belongs to the red cultural group. Otherwise, it belongs to the green one.

In the simulations in Chapter 2, we assumed that an agents' preferences depended on the relationship, at any given time, between their sugar stock relative to their metabolic need for sugar, versus their spice stock relative to their metabolic need for spice. Now we will assume that the preferences of the agents also depend on their cultural attribute. Specifically, we will assume that they depend on the value of f, the fraction of R labels in the label string. That is to say that their cultural inclination (more toward the red culture or more toward the green one) will affect their preferences. But let us remember that due to the process of cultural influence that occurs in exchange meetings, the cultural labels of each agent will change, and therefore the value of f will also change. In other words, we are facing a model in which preferences change endogenously, as a result of inter-actions between agents.[4]

Figure 8.1 shows the evolution of the average exchange price throughout a simulation of 100 periods, and where the initial conditions (agents' vision, metabolisms, initial endowments, and the geography of the Sugarscape) are the same as in the Chapter 2 experiment whose results are shown in Figure 2.9. We can see that in the experiment shown in Figure 8.1 the average price follows what seems to be a random walk, unlike the case in the experiment in Chapter 2 in which prices fluctuated around a value near one. This should not surprise us, since here agents' preferences are constant-ly changing as a result of the process of cultural change.[5]

Let us now look at other examples. In Chapter 7, we saw an artificial game that played out in a two-dimensional cellular automaton. Each agent (each player) had a very simple rule of conduct: it started the game with a given behavior (it cooperated or defected) and after each round of games against its neighbors it adopted as its own the strategy that gave the best result. In other words, its behavior changed as a result of interaction with other agents. Likewise, in Chapter 3, we saw a more complex artificial game. Remember that it was an evolutionary game in which successive generations of artificial agents evolved according to the game strategies coded on their chromosomes, and where those strategies were, in fact, their

---

[4] Recall that in Chapter 2 the preferences of each agent are represented with a welfare function W as follows:

$$W(w_{sp}, w_{sp}) = w_{su}^{m_{su}/m_T} w_{sp}^{m_{sp}/m_T}$$

where w_{su} is the amount of sugar that the agent has accumulated and w_{sp} that of spice, m_{su} is its metabolic sugar need, and m_{sp} that of spice, and where $m_T = m_{su} + m_{sp}$. Suppose f is the fraction of tags equal to R in the agent tag string, and enter it into the welfare function W as follows:

$$W(w_{su}, w_{sp}) = w_{su}^{(m_{su}/m_T)f} w_{sp}^{(m_{sp}/m_T)(1-f)}$$

where m_T is now:

$$m_T = m_{su}f + m_{sp}(1 - f)$$

Since f changes throughout the simulation, consequently the welfare function represent-ing the preferences of the agents also changes.

[5] For analyses of the coevolution of institutions and preferences that combine mathematical modeling with AE models, see Bowles (2003).

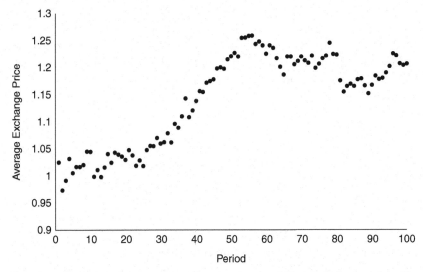

Figure 8.1 Evolution of the average exchange price over 100 periods for a model with endogenous preferences

rules of behavior. In that evolutionary game each agent played the prisoner's dilemma against each of its opponents twenty times. And its strategy of play, that is, its behavior, was coded on a ten-gene chromosome. For example, a chromosome like the following meant that the artificial agent's behavior was always to defect:

1111111111

while a chromosome like the following:

1111100000

meant that the agent had the strategy of defecting five times and then cooperating five times.

Unlike the game presented in Chapter 3, let's say now that after each round of games, each agent observes and copies the two most successful strategies (the ones that earned the highest sum of payoffs) and that it uses those strategies as "parent" strategies to generate its new strategy. To do this, it crosses over the chromosomes of those two strategies, and then introduces a random mutation into one of its genes, thus obtaining its new strategy to apply in the next round of games. In short, instead of seeing the game, as we did in Chapter 3, as the evolution of a changing population of agents in which some die and others are born, we now see it as one in which what evolves are the strategies of the agents (i.e., their rules of behavior).

As we also saw in Chapter 3, the collective result of the individual behaviors deployed by artificial agents in the prisoner's dilemma game is that the social structure, initially made up of individuals with different rules of behavior, converges to a society in which all its members are defectors. That is, it becomes a homogeneous society.

What is surprising, as we saw in that game, is that a society in which everyone is a defector gets a worse result than it would if everyone cooperated. Moreover, even if all players were aware of this absurdity, the incentives of the game are such that the only rational option remains to defect. However, this could be mitigated or resolved if a social norm or institution were imposed that forced agents to cooperate, either because some punishment mechanism is implemented for those who do not co-operate, or because agents end up internalizing such a norm as a new rule of behavior. There are indeed social norms and institutions that owe their genesis, dissemination, and continuity to the fact that they contribute to improving social welfare. This is another kind of interesting experiment that can be carried out in an artificial economy.

Remember that in Chapter 2 we presented two different artificial agents' interaction models. In one, they followed a movement rule, collecting the resources found in their neighborhoods, storing them and consuming what was necessary to survive. In the other, in addition to following the movement rule, agents followed a trade rule: they exchanged resources with their neighbors, according to their preferences and resource availability.

Suppose we simulate both types of models, each with agent populations with the same basic characteristics – that is, the same ranges of vision and metabolism – and that they live within identical geographies in terms of resource availability. And suppose we compute the number of agents that survive after some time.

Figure 8.2 shows the result of this experiment. We can see that starting from an initial population of 759 agents (panel a), the number that survives after 50 periods and when there is trade is equal to 241 (panel b), while when there is not trade it is equal to 137 (panel c). In other words, in the Sugarscape, trade, where it exists, is superior to the case in which it does not exist, since agents that did not have the necessary resources to survive (the minimum amounts of sugar and spice necessary to satisfy their metabolism) can now obtain them. Thus, the population that can be kept alive is greater because of the existence of a new economic institution: the market.

The previous examples do not cover, of course, all the possible ways of computationally modeling some aspects of the agent/structure problem.

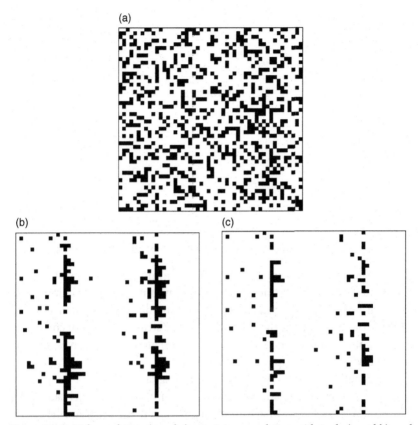

Figure 8.2 Initial population (panel a), surviving population with trade (panel b), and surviving population without trade (panel c), after 50 periods

But they let us see that AE allows us to use sophisticated computational tools to address important problems such as the change in individual attributes and behaviors as a result of economic interactions and the economic effects of introducing social norms or institutions. These achievements do not exhaust the challenge of developing an intermediate stance on the agent/structure problem, in which agents and structures are generated reciprocally and dynamically, since this also requires models capable of endogenously generating both economic institutions, as well as mechanisms for the transmission and internalization of norms of behavior at the level of individual agents.[6] But for what we have seen, AE presents an interesting research program in that regard.

[6] For an introductory book on modeling norms, see Elsenbroich and Gilbert (2013). See also Newmann (2008), Hollander and Wu (2011), Squazzoni (2012), and Villatoro et al. (2015).

Annexes

Annex A Notions about Object-Oriented Programming

There are various paradigms and programming methods suitable for different types of applications. The programming and simulation of an artificial economy can be carried out with standard methods, or through object-oriented programming, which is a very structured way of constructing computational objects, which are encapsulated in themselves, but can interact with other computational objects.

The generic structure (what in programming jargon is called the pseudo-code) of an object-oriented computer program of an AE model can be described as follows. First, we have the main program. In this program, the agents' population is initialized, setting the number of agents, and giving values to their individual characteristics. Then agents are made interact repeatedly (e.g., exchanging goods), to finally compute a set of statistics (such as the quantities exchanged, prices, the distribution of income, etc.).

Typical Main Program of an AE Model

```
Initialization of agent and population variables;
Repeat the following two sentences n times:
        Interaction of agents;
        Cumulative computation of population statistics;
End;
```

Each agent is represented as a computational object, which is in fact a relatively independent piece of programming code that can be used by the main program. Each agent has states (represented by variables that contain data) and rules of behavior (called methods, procedures, or functions). Their states and behaviors can be of private or public access (when they can be seen and used by other agents).

Object Agent

```
Private variables:
Preferences; Wealth;
...
Public variables:
Supply price; Demand price;
Supply quantity; Demand quantity;
...
Private behaviors:
Calculation of valuations based on preferences, prices, and
quantities;
...
Public behaviors:
Search for agents to carry out exchanges;
Communication with agents to carry out exchanges;
...
End;
```

The population of agents is also considered as an object that has states (data related to agents) and functions and methods (used to compute population statistics).

Object Population

```
Private variables:
Active representation of the population;
Currently active agent;
...
Public variables:
Number of agents; Prices; Quantities of goods;
...
Private behaviors:
Generate initial population randomly;
Accumulate in global statistics the characteristics of each
agent;
...
Public behaviors:
```

```
Compute average price for each commodity;
...
End;
```

When the program is executed, the interactions between agents can be simulated as occurring simultaneously or sequentially, and the temporality of them implicitly defines a global clock and what is defined as a period in the model.

Among the computer languages for object-oriented programming are Java, C^{++}, and others. Also, MATLAB and Mathematica allow programming in this way. NetLogo is an entry-level multi-agent programmable modeling environment that shares many features with object-oriented programming languages. For references on specialized software for AE models, see the website created and maintained by Leigh Tesfatsion at: www2.econ.iastate.edu/tesfatsi/ace.htm

Annex B Mainstream Economics: A Brief on Its Theoretical Core

It can be said that the theoretical core of ME is made up of the general equilibrium theory and classical game theory. It is a strongly axiomatized core, of great sophistication and formal elegance.

Regarding general equilibrium theory, the Walras-Arrow-Debreu model is the most sophisticated theoretical and instrumental reference.[1] It allows the study of a specific type of social interaction between agents: a competitive market equilibrium. An equilibrium is a situation that tends to reproduce over time without changes, given that no agent has incentives to alter it.

Agents are defined as decision units which optimize the satisfaction of their preferences given their resource constraints. Each agent has a set of preferences on all existing goods and services not only at a given moment, but also through time, and in all possible states of nature; it is an insatiable being, because it always prefers more to equal or less; it is selfish, because it seeks to satisfy its individual preferences; it is rational, because it makes transitive and complete choices,[2] which allows building an ordinal utility function to represent them; and it is a price-taker, that is, an infinitesimal

---

[1] The canonical texts are Gerard Debreu (1972), and Arrow and Hahn (1983). Most microeconomics textbooks contain introductory notions to the theory of partial and general equilibrium.

[2] In most ME models it is also assumed, implicitly or explicitly, that agents are fully rational (i.e., they have an unlimited capacity of gathering and processing information).

force that cannot significantly influence either the individual behavior of other agents or their overall result.

Agents are seen from a behaviorist point of view, as their preferences and decision mechanisms are inferred from their manifest behavior (doctrine of revealed preference) without postulating or elucidating the existence and functioning of mental phenomena. Likewise, social interaction is limited to market interactions. The market is basically the only existing social institution.

Many economic models widely used are obtained as particularizations of the Walras-Arrow-Debreu model, ranging from static and deterministic to intertemporal and uncertain. Among these models we can mention partial equilibrium, Ramsey-Cass-Koopmans, dynamic stochastic general equilibrium, and others.[3]

Walras-Arrow-Debreu is, in a way, a case of the theory of noncooperative games. In this theory, the assumption of price-taking as a characteristic of individual behavior is replaced by the strategic interaction between agents. Now each agent must anticipate the strategies of the others. Thus, individual expectations and behaviors have an impact on the overall result, that is, on the equilibrium of the game. There are several equilibrium concepts in the field of noncooperative game theory. The main ones are those of dominance (when one strategy is better than any other strategy for one player, regardless of how the other players may play) and Nash equilibrium (when expectations and actions of all players are mutually compatible, and there are no incentives to change actions), to which a series of refinements is applied.[4]

Besides noncooperative games, there are cooperative games, in which agents can collude to optimize their payoffs. Within cooperative games there are also several concepts of equilibrium, such as core, von Neumann-Morgenstern stable set, nucleolus, and Shapley value, which predict the formation of coalitions and the distribution of payoffs.

Noncooperative and cooperative games constitute classical game theory, which includes static games (the game is played once and players move simultaneously), sequential games (players make moves at different times or in turns), repeated games (the same game is played over and over for a given number of periods), and dynamic games (strategic interactions among players recur over time, and decisions made during one period

---

[3] To perform normative analysis, a specific field of welfare economics, a welfare function is added to these models, but this implies cardinalizing the utility function.

[4] The pioneering canonical text of game theory is von Neumann and Morgenstern (2007). Another reference text is Fudenberg and Tirole (1991). Most textbooks of microeconomics and game theory provide introductory notions to classical game theory.

affect not only the current payoffs but also the future ones),[5] with complete or incomplete information. From these games result not only price and quantity equilibria as in Walras-Arrow-Debreu, but also equilibria (solutions) that can be interpreted as institutions (i.e., mechanisms that give a lasting structure to social interactions). Institutional change can be thought of as a passage from one equilibrium to another in a game of multiple equilibria. Alternatively, the games themselves can also be interpreted as institutions (rules of the game), and institutional change as the passage from one game to another.

Having briefly reviewed the most general theoretical core of ME, we will look at some definitional and methodological issues. It is interesting to note that ME defines its field of study in terms of causal factors with which it is concerned, not in terms of a specific domain or realm (Hausman, 1992). Indeed, ME claims that it studies rational, optimizing, and selfish individual actions, under resource constraints, and the coordination of these actions. Traditionally, ME focused on the study of these topics in typical economic subfields such as markets of goods, labor markets, finance, etc. But more recently it expanded its scope to include demographic, sociological, political, psychological, and other fields, showing an "imperialist" behavior.

ME contrasts with the way in which the fields of study of other social and human sciences are defined. Usually, the definition and separation of those sciences is made in terms of substantive fields: medicine studies the human body, neuroscience the brain, psychology the mind, anthropology studies primitive societies, and sociology contemporary societies. Within the realm of economics, classical political economy and Marxist political economy, for example, study the processes and institutions linked to the production, distribution, and consumption, of goods and some types of services (commercial, financial, and others). However, as we saw previously, with ME something different happens.

Annex C General Equilibrium: Static and Dynamic Models

In this Annex, we present in detail the mathematical representations of the static and dynamic general equilibrium models of Chapter 2. The pioneering work in general equilibrium modeling was carried out by Leon Walras in 1874, and hence such models are known as Walrasian general

---

[5] Dynamic games are also known as differential games, which are cases of optimal control models.

equilibrium models; their modern mathematical formulation was developed in the 1950s by Kenneth Arrow, Gerard Debreu, and Lionel McKenzie.

A general equilibrium model is a mathematical representation of market interactions between many consumers and firms, which determines the quantities of commodities supplied and demanded, and their prices. It is often assumed that perfect competition prevails in all markets: the number of participants is so large that none has a significant influence on the behavior of the economy (i.e., on the prices and quantities of goods produced, exchanged, and consumed).

Given a set of utility functions that characterize consumer preferences, a set of production functions that characterize the technologies that firms have access to, and a set of initial resource endowments, a general equilibrium is characterized by three fundamental features:

1. All consumers maximize utility.
2. All firms maximize profits.
3. There is a set of prices at which all markets clear (i.e., supply and demand equalize, so there is no excess demand or supply).

It should be mentioned that only under some restrictive conditions is the set of general equilibrium prices and quantities unique and stable.

Depending on the interpretation of the concept of commodity, a general equilibrium model can be extended in different directions. To do this, in addition to their intrinsic properties, commodities can be distinguished by their spatial location, their temporal location, and by the state of nature. Thus, if we consider a commodity in two different places as if they were two different commodities, we can build a spatial economy model; if we consider a commodity at two different times as if they were two different commodities, we can build a dynamic model; and if we consider a commodity in two possible states of the world as if they were two different commodities, we can build a stochastic model. Of course, we can also combine these interpretations. For example, if we consider a commodity in different places, times, and states of the world, as if they were several different commodities, we can build a spatial dynamic stochastic model.

C.1 Static Exchange Model

In this section, we present the mathematical representation of the static exchange general equilibrium model seen in Chapter 2. For the purpose of simplifying, we use only two agents and two goods, but the model and results are easily generalized to any number of agents and goods.[6]

There are two agents, A and B, who exchange two goods, sugar (su) and spice (sp), whose prices are, respectively, p_{su} and p_{sp}. Each agent has an initial endowment of sugar and spice: w_{su}^A and w_{sp}^A for agent A, w_{su}^B and w_{sp}^B for B. Each agent's preferences are represented by a utility function: $u^A(x_{su}^A, x_{sp}^A)$ for A and $u^B(x_{su}^B, x_{sp}^B)$ for B, where x_{su}^A, x_{sp}^A, x_{su}^B, x_{sp}^B are the quantities of sugar and spice.

Each agent maximizes utility subject to its budget constraint, which is given by the wealth it owns (m^A and m^B). This wealth is equal to the value of its initial sugar and spice endowments, that is, their quantities valued at their respective prices. With its wealth the agent can buy an equivalent value of goods. Thus, for agent A we have:

$$\text{maximize} \quad u^A(x_{su}^A, x_{sp}^A) \tag{C.1}$$

$$\text{subject to:} \ p_{su}\,x_{su}^A + p_{sp}\,x_{sp}^A = p_{su}w_{su}^A + p_{sp}w_{sp}^A = m^A \tag{C.2}$$

while for agent B:

$$\text{maximize} \quad u^B(x_{su}^B, x_{sp}^B) \tag{C.3}$$

$$\text{subject to:} \ p_{su}\,x_{su}^B + p_{sp}\,x_{sp}^B = p_{su}\,w_{su}^B + p_{sp}\,w_{sp}^B = m^B \tag{C.4}$$

From the solution of these maximization problems, we obtain the demands of each good by each agent, which are functions of prices and wealth.

$$x_{su}^A(p_{su}, p_{sp}, m^A) \tag{C.5}$$

$$x_{sp}^A(p_{su}, p_{sp}, m^A) \tag{C.6}$$

$$x_{su}^B(p_{su}, p_{sp}, m^B) \tag{C.7}$$

$$x_{sp}^B(p_{su}, p_{sp}, m^B) \tag{C.8}$$

The total, or aggregate demand, of each good is the sum of the demands of the two agents.

---

[6] Presentations of these kinds of models are in almost all advanced microeconomics textbooks, and in some of intermediate microeconomics.

$$x_{su} = x_{su}^A + x_{su}^B \tag{C.9}$$

$$x_{sp} = x_{sp}^A + x_{sp}^B \tag{C.10}$$

Aggregate supply is equal to the sum of the initial endowments of each good.

$$w_{su} = w_{su}^A + w_{su}^B \tag{C.11}$$

$$w_{sp} = w_{sp}^A + w_{sp}^B \tag{C.12}$$

Finally, a market clearing condition is imposed which states that aggregate demand and aggregate supply of each good are equal.

$$x_{su} = w_{su} \tag{C.13}$$

$$x_{sp} = w_{sp} \tag{C.14}$$

To obtain an example like the one presented in Chapter 2, assume the utility functions are of the Cobb–Douglass form.

$$u^A = \left(x_{su}^A\right)^{\alpha^A} \left(x_{sp}^A\right)^{1-\alpha^A} \tag{C.15}$$

$$u^B = \left(x_{su}^B\right)^{\alpha^B} \left(x_{sp}^B\right)^{1-\alpha^B} \tag{C.16}$$

From utility maximization according to equations (C.1), (C.2), (C.3) and (C.4), and using the forms of the utility function given by equations (C.15) and (C.16), we obtain the demand functions for each good, by each agent.

$$x_{su}^A = \frac{\alpha^A\, m^A}{P_{su}} = \frac{\alpha^A \left(P_{su}\, w_{su}^A + P_{sp}\, w_{sp}^A\right)}{P_{su}} \tag{C.17}$$

$$x_{sp}^A = \frac{\left(1 - \alpha^A\right) m^A}{P_{sp}} = \frac{\left(1 - \alpha^A\right) \left(P_{su}\, w_{su}^A + P_{sp}\, w_{sp}^A\right)}{P_{sp}} \tag{C.18}$$

$$x_{su}^B = \frac{\alpha^B\, m^B}{P_{su}} = \frac{\alpha^B \left(P_{su}\, w_{su}^B + P_{sp}\, w_{sp}^B\right)}{P_{su}} \tag{C.19}$$

$$x_{sp}^B = \frac{\left(1 - \alpha^B\right) m^B}{P_{sp}} = \frac{\left(1 - \alpha^B\right) \left(P_{su}\, w_{su}^B + P_{sp}\, w_{sp}^B\right)}{P_{sp}} \tag{C.20}$$

If, in accordance with equations (C.13) and (C.14), we equalize the aggregate demand to the aggregate supply of each good, we get a two-equation system that represents our small static general equilibrium model.

$$\frac{\alpha^A \left(p_{su}\, w_{su}^A + p_{sp}\, w_{sp}^A\right)}{p_{su}} + \frac{\alpha^B \left(p_{su}\, w_{su}^B + p_{sp}\, w_{sp}^B\right)}{p_{su}} = w_{su}^A + w_{su}^B \quad (C.21)$$

$$\frac{(1-\alpha^A) \left(p_{su}\, w_{su}^A + p_{sp}\, w_{sp}^A\right)}{p_{sp}} + \frac{(1-\alpha^B) \left(p_{su}\, w_{su}^B + p_{sp}\, w_{sp}^B\right)}{p_{sp}} = w_{sp}^A + w_{sp}^B$$

$$(C.22)$$

Suppose that the values of the coefficients of the utility functions are symmetrical and the initial endowments of goods are equal, and that their values are as follows: $\alpha^A = 0.25$, $\alpha^B = 0.75$ and $m_{su}^A = m_{sp}^A = m_{su}^B = m_{sp}^B = 25$. Also, let us choose as numeraire the price of spice, that is, $p_{sp} = 1$. If we replace these values in equations (C.21) and (C.22), we get that in general equilibrium the price of sugar in terms of spice is $p_{su} = 1$, that the aggregate demand and supply of sugar are equal to 50, and that the aggregate demand and supply of spice are also equal to 50. If we plot the functions of aggregate demand and supply of sugar, we obtain the sugar market chart shown in Chapter 2, Figure 2.13.

C.2 Dynamic Production and Consumption Model

In this section, we present the mathematical representation of the dynamic general equilibrium model with production and consumption seen in Chapter 2. It is a typical ME model used to mathematically represent processes of economic growth, and is known as the Ramsey-Cass-Koopmans model, since it was created by Frank Ramsey in 1928, and then expanded and perfected by David Cass and Tjalling Koopmans in 1965.[7] Interestingly, it was initially formulated as a centralized economic planning model, and then adopted as a decentralized market economy model, as it can be demonstrated that under some conditions centralized and decentralized solutions are equivalent. It is also used as the basis for the formulation of long-run intertemporal growth models, and in short- and medium-run macroeconomic applications in the form of stochastic dynamic general equilibrium models.

---

[7] Presentations of this kind of model are found in almost all advanced macroeconomics textbooks.

As we did in Chapter 2, we assume that the economy is made of two representative agents: a household and a firm, and that both live infinitely. The household seeks to maximize its intertemporal well-being function W throughout its life (i.e., between period zero and infinity). This results in maximizing utility $u(C_t)$ it gets from consumption in each period. We assume that the household values a unit of consumption today more than a unit of consumption in the future. As a result, each future period is discounted with a discount factor $e^{-\rho t}$ with a time preference rate ρ, which implies that as time goes on $u(C_t)$ is divided by an ever-larger number.

$$W = \int_{t=0}^{\infty} u(C_t)\, e^{-\rho t} dt \qquad (C.23)$$

To achieve its goal, the household faces a budget constraint given by the change in the assets A_t it owns in each period. These assets evolve over time according to the following differential equation, which tells us that the increase in A in period t, that is $\dot{A}_t$, is equal to wage income (W_t) plus rent from assets (which is equal to the stock of assets A_t multiplied by the interest rate r_t), minus consumption (C_t).

$$\dot{A}_t = W_t + r_t A_t - C_t \qquad (C.24)$$

Firm's profit (π_t) in each period is equal to income minus cost. Income is equal to the value of production, which is undertaken using capital (K_t) and labor (L_t) as production factors, combining them according to a particular technology, which we represent mathematically through the production function $F(K_t, L_t)$. Costs are equal to rent payments for household-owned capital use plus wage payments for labor, that is also provided by households.

$$\pi_t = F(K_t, L_t) - r_t K_t - W_t L_t \qquad (C.25)$$

The firm seeks to maximize the present value of profits throughout its life. In this model, this is equivalent to maximizing profit in each period. Since we assume that all markets operate in perfect competition, then the interest rate is equal to the marginal productivity of capital.

$$r_t = F'(K_t, L_t) \qquad (C.26)$$

Normalizing $L_t = 1$, the wage is equal to:

$$W_t = F(K_t, L_t) - K_t F'(K_t, L_t) \tag{C.27}$$

That is to say that wages are obtained as the difference between the value of the product of the firm and capital income, since in perfect competition the sum of wage and capital income is equal to the value of the product. Since the household is the owner of the capital that the firm rents, then household assets are equal to the capital stock of the economy.

$$A_t = K_t \tag{C.28}$$

The solution of the model is the system of two differential equations shown here, which characterizes its dynamic.

$$r_t = \rho - \left(\frac{u''(C_t)\ C_t}{u'(C_t)} \right) \frac{\dot{C}_t}{C_t} \tag{C.29}$$

$$\dot{K}_t = F(K_t, L_t) - C_t - K_t \tag{C.30}$$

To these equations we must add a transversality condition that states that the value of household assets goes to zero as time goes to infinity.[8] This means that the household does not keep any valuable assets at the end of its life but consumes everything.

$$\lim_{t \to \infty} (V_t A_t) = 0 \tag{C.31}$$

Suppose that the utility of consumption in each period takes the functional form known as constant elasticity of substitution, where such elasticity is given by the inverse of the θ parameter.

$$u(C_t) = \frac{(C_t)^{1-\theta} - 1}{1 - \theta} \tag{C.32}$$

Let us also assume that the production function takes the functional form known as Cobb–Douglass with constant returns to scale (the exponents of capital and labor add up to one), and where the α parameter represents the share of capital in the product of the economy.

---

[8] The value of household assets is equal to the present value of the shadow price of income (V_t) multiplied by the amount of assets (A_t). The shadow price of income is a variable that arises from mathematically solving the problem of household maximization, which is a problem of intertemporal optimization.

$$F(K_t, L_t) = K_t^\alpha \, L_t^{1-\alpha} \tag{C.33}$$

So, the system of differential equations that characterizes the dynamics of the economy becomes:

$$\frac{\dot{C}_t}{C_t} = \frac{1}{\theta}(r_t - \rho) \tag{C.34}$$

$$\dot{K}_t = K_t^\alpha L_t^{1-\alpha} - C_t - K_t \tag{C.35}$$

to which we must add, as above, the same transversality condition. The qualitative dynamics of this general equilibrium model is usually represented in a phase or space diagram like the one shown in Figure Annex C.1, the simplified version of which we presented in Chapter 2, Figure 2.18.

Each point in the diagram represents a joint state of capital and consumption, and each curve represents a joint path of capital and consumption (i.e., their transitions between states). There are infinite possible paths, and each is a solution of the system of differential equations that characterizes the dynamic of the system from given initial conditions for capital and consumption. In the figure we only show some representative paths.

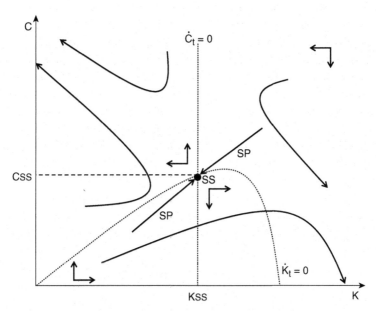

Figure Annex C.1 Phase diagram of the joint evolution of consumption and the capital stock in the dynamic production and consumption model

We can see that there are two demarcation lines: one vertical, that contains the states of the system in which consumption growth is equal to zero ($\dot{C}_t = 0$), and another that starts from the origin of the coordinate system and contains the states in which the growth of capital is equal to zero ($\dot{K}_t = 0$). The intersection of both lines gives us a steady state (SS) of the system, through which passes only one curve (SP) called saddle path, given by the path that converges toward the steady state from the southwest and from the northeast. The four pairs of orthogonal arrows (i.e., perpendicular to each other) indicate the directions of movement in the subspaces of the phase diagram bounded by the demarcation lines.

If we add to the production function a stock of technology as another factor of production, if we assume that such technology takes the Harrod-neutral form (i.e., it increases the efficiency of labor), and if we assume a constant growth rate for that stock, the steady state ceases to characterize a state of rest of the system, and becomes a state of balanced growth, where model variables such as production, consumption, capital stock, and wages, all grow at the same constant rate, equal to the growth rate of the stock of technology. In other words, the pace of technological progress becomes the fundamental determinant of the economy's growth in the long run. In the growth chart presented in Chapter 2, Figure 2.17, we can observe the trajectories of the product, consumption, capital, salary, and interest rate, when we simulate this model for the following parameter values: $\theta = 0.9$, $\rho = 0.03$, $\alpha = 0.75$, $K_0 = 0.1$, and a growth rate of technological progress of 2 percent per period.

As we saw in the phase diagram in Chapter 2, Figure 2.18, given an initial condition for capital, for the system to converge toward the steady state (or, as we mentioned previously, toward a balanced growth path), and not to experience catastrophic dynamics, the only possibility is that consumption ends up exactly on the saddle path. This is achieved if and only if the transversality condition that we saw earlier in equation (C.31) is met, which forces consumption to "jump" immediately over the saddle path whatever the initial level of the capital stock. A highly demanding condition for the household deciding on the level of consumption, requiring full rationality (i.e., an unlimited capacity to gather and process information) since, of all possible paths of the economic system, it must choose exactly that.

Annex D Artificial Neural Networks: A Brief on Models and Learning

In Chapter 1, we introduced the basic concepts of artificial neural networks, and in Chapter 5, we presented a very simple model and a

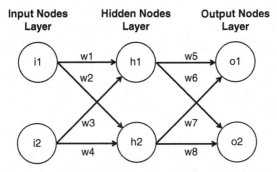

Figure Annex D.1 Feedforward artificial neural network

rudimentary example of network learning. Here we will introduce slightly more complex models, a more sophisticated learning mechanism, and some general considerations about artificial neural networks.[9]

Figure Annex D.1 shows an artificial neural network composed of two input nodes, two hidden nodes, and two output nodes. This model is known as feedforward model, since information flows straight from the inputs to the hidden nodes then to the output nodes. That is, connections between nodes do not form a cycle.

The input layer may contain, for example, data on the money supply and government expenditure, while the output layer data may correspond to the gross domestic product and the price level. The first step in training this network consists of a forward pass. Starting from the input nodes, the corresponding values of the combination function of each hidden node are computed. For the hidden node 1, we have:

$$h_{1c} = i_1 \, w_1 + i_2 \, w_2 \qquad (D.1)$$

and for the hidden node 2:

$$h_{2c} = i_1 \, w_3 + i_2 \, w_4 \qquad (D.2)$$

With these values, the corresponding values of the activation functions are computed. Unlike the example introduced in Chapter 5, where the activation function was a threshold function, here we will apply a more commonly used type of function: the logistic function, whose mathematical expression is:

---

[9] For a systematic presentation of models and learning methods, see Haykin (2009). For a computational implementation of a simple artificial neural network to predict a stock market price see Kendrick, Mercado, and Amman (2006), pp. 25–36.

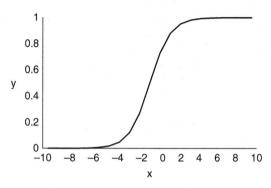

Figure Annex D.2 Logistic function

$$y = \frac{1}{1 + e^{-x}} \tag{D.3}$$

This function constraints the activation function to take values between 0 and 1, as shown in Figure Annex D.2.[10]

The activation functions corresponding to the hidden nodes 1 and 2 are thus the following ones:

$$h_{1a} = \frac{1}{1 + e^{-h_{1c}}} \tag{D.4}$$

$$h_{2a} = \frac{1}{1 + e^{-h_{2c}}} \tag{D.5}$$

The next step is to compute the combination functions of the output nodes.

$$o_{1c} = h_{1a}w_5 + h_{2a}w_6 \tag{D.6}$$

$$o_{2c} = h_{1a}w_7 + h_{2a}w_8 \tag{D.7}$$

The value of the combination functions of the output nodes are the predicted values generated by the artificial neural network, given its inputs. Finally, we compute the prediction errors, that is, the differences between

---

[10] Usually, a bias parameter is also included in the combination function of each hidden or output node of the artificial neural network. Its role is analog to the one of a constant term in a linear function, allowing the prediction of the artificial neural network to be more precise. The bias term shifts the combination function, hence the activation function, to the left or right (if a logistic function is used, it changes the steepness of the function). Usually, the value of the bias term is set equal to 1, and it is multiplied by a weight.

the predicted values o_{1c} and o_{2c} and the actual output values o_1 and o_2. These errors are fed into an error function, which usually takes the form of a quadratic expression like the following:

$$J = \frac{1}{2}\left\{(o_1 - o_{1c})^2 + (o_2 - o_{2c})^2\right\} \tag{D.8}$$

With this we finish the first forward pass to train the artificial neural network. The next step is to update the network weights to reduce the prediction errors. To do so, we apply the backpropagation method, which uses a gradient descent algorithm. This algorithm is an iterative procedure to find the minimum of a function, taking steps proportional to the negative of the gradient of the function. The gradient can be interpreted as the tangent vector at a given point of the function that gives the direction and rate of fastest increase. In our example, the gradient of the J function is:

$$\nabla J = \begin{bmatrix} \dfrac{\partial J}{\partial w_1} \\ \vdots \\ \dfrac{\partial J}{\partial w_8} \end{bmatrix} \tag{D.9}$$

The updating rule for each weight is:

$$w.new = w - \alpha\,\frac{\partial J}{\partial w} \tag{D.10}$$

where α is a parameter named learning rate, whose value is usually set between 0 and 1. To obtain the value of each partial derivative, we apply the chain rule. For example, for the output layer node number one and weight number five:

$$\frac{\partial J}{\partial w_5} = \frac{\partial J}{\partial o_{1c}}\frac{\partial o_{1c}}{\partial w_5} \tag{D.11}$$

and for the hidden layer node number one and weight number one:[11]

$$\frac{\partial J}{\partial w_1} = \frac{\partial h_{1a}}{\partial h_{1c}}\frac{\partial h_{1c}}{\partial w_1}\left(\frac{\partial J}{\partial o_{1c}}\frac{\partial o_{1c}}{\partial h_{1a}} + \frac{\partial J}{\partial o_{2c}}\frac{\partial o_{2c}}{\partial h_{1a}}\right) \tag{D.12}$$

---

[11] If bias terms are included in the combination functions of the network nodes, their weights will be updated in the gradient descent algorithm in an analogous way as the other weights (i.e., as a function of the partial derivative of the error function with respect to the bias weight).

Once the weights have been updated, the forward pass is repeated to obtain new output predicted values. These values are fed into the error function, and the backpropagation method is applied again to obtain new values for the weights, and so on until the error function value is as small as a given tolerance value.

The learning example that we have presented corresponds to a single training example, made up of two input values and two output values. But usually, the training of an artificial neural network is done with a set of many examples. Suppose that we now have two training examples named 1 and 2: $(i_1^1, i_2^1, o_1^1, o_2^1)$ and $(i_1^2, i_2^2, o_1^2, o_2^2)$, where the superscript indicates the example number. Thus, we must perform a forward pass for each one, in order to obtain the corresponding predictions. Then, the error function becomes:

$$J = \frac{1}{2}\{(o_1^1 - o_{1c}^1)^2 + (o_2^1 - o_{2c}^1)^2 + (o_1^2 - o_{1c}^2)^2 + (o_2^2 - o_{2c}^2)^2\} \quad\quad (D.13)$$

The updating rule for the weights remains the same, as does the backpropagation method and the gradient descent algorithm. But there are two methods of iteration: with an "on-line" method, we proceed to repeat the previous steps for each example; with an "off-line" method, we update the weights for all the examples at once. In this case, we will have more equations for the combination functions of the output layer:

$$o_{2c}^1 = h_{1a}^1 \, w_5 + h_{2a}^1 w_6 \quad\quad (D.14)$$

$$o_{2c}^1 = h_{1a}^1 \, w_7 + h_{2a}^1 w_8 \qu\quad (D.15)$$

$$o_{1c}^2 = h_{1a}^2 \, w_5 + h_{2a}^2 w_6 \qu\quad (D.16)$$

$$o_{1c}^2 = h_{1a}^2 \, w_5 + h_{2a}^2 w_6 \qu\quad (D.17)$$

and, in a similar fashion, we will have more equations for the activation functions of the hidden layer nodes:

$$h_{1a}^1 = \frac{1}{1 + e^{h_{1c}^1}} \qu\quad (D.18)$$

$$h_{2a}^1 = \frac{1}{1 + e^{h_{2c}^1}} \qu\quad (D.19)$$

$$h_{1a}^2 = \frac{1}{1 + e^{h_{1c}^2}} \qquad (D.20)$$

$$h_{2a}^2 = \frac{1}{1 + e^{h_{2c}^2}} \qquad (D.21)$$

and also, for the combination functions of the hidden layer nodes:

$$h_{1c}^1 = i_1^1 \, w_1 + i_2^1 \, w_2 \qquad (D.22)$$

$$h_{2c}^1 = i_1^1 \, w_3 + i_2^1 \, w_4 \qquad (D.23)$$

$$h_{1c}^2 = i_1^2 \, w_1 + i_2^2 \, w_2 \qquad (D.24)$$

$$h_{2c}^2 = i_1^2 \, w_3 + i_2^2 \, w_4 \qquad (D.25)$$

There are network architectures other than the feedforward model dealt with here. For example, unlike a feedforward network in which we input data at the same time, and they flow to the output layer, in a recurrent neural network architecture previous outputs can be used as inputs. A simple recurrent neural network model is shown in Figure Annex D.3.

In a recurrent network, data are input sequentially. In our simple example, we input i1 first, then we input i2 to the result of inputting i1, then we input i3 to the result of inputting i2. Thus, we have an order in time between the data, and there is a dependence between current information and previous information. For example, we may have a time series of data

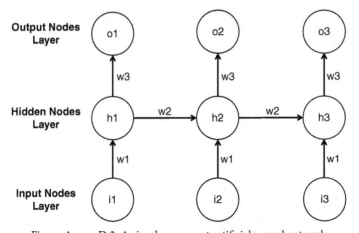

Figure Annex D.3 A simple recurrent artificial neural network

on the gross domestic product of an economy, and using those data we may want to predict its future evolution. One of the advantages of this network architecture is that, given its sequential nature, it can deal with sets of data of variable length.

If we want to obtain the mathematical representation of our model, for the combination function of the second output node we will have:

$$o_{2c} = h_{2a} w_3 \tag{D.26}$$

while for activation function of the second hidden node, if we use a logistic function:

$$h_{2a} = \frac{1}{1 + e^{-h_{2c}}} \tag{D.27}$$

and for the combination function:

$$h_{2c} = i_2 w_1 + h_{1a} w_2 \tag{D.28}$$

In a similar fashion we can obtain the equations for the other output and hidden nodes. There are variations of recurrent networks. For example, hidden nodes may contain a feedback loop: the output of the activation function is used, with a time delay, as an input to the same node. Or output nodes may become input nodes: the value of the output node is used as the next input node of the network. Feedforward networks and recurrent networks do not exhaust the universe of network architectures. On the contrary, this universe keeps expanding with diverse types of networks each suitable for specific applications.[12]

We presented examples with a single hidden layer. However, artificial neural networks can have many hidden layers. When that is the case, we say that the network implements a process of deep learning, using multiple layers to progressively extract higher-level features from its raw inputs, that is, each level learns to transform its input data into a more abstract and composite representation.[13] For instance, when an artificial neural network is used for image processing, its lower layers may identify edges, while higher layers may identify faces. Moreover, an artificial neural network can have not only many layers, but also many nodes in each layer. The exponential growth in computer power has made it possible to implement

---

[12] For an overview of many alternative network architectures, see the compilation made by van Veen (2017).

[13] For a systematic presentation of deep learning, see Goodfellow, Bengio, and Courville (2016).

networks with millions of nodes. Thus, an artificial neural network can be seen as a massively parallel distributed processor built with simple processing units capable of storing and using knowledge, where by knowledge we mean information used by the network to interpret and predict its environment. The network acquires knowledge by means of its learning algorithm, while the interconnections between its nodes (the weights) store that knowledge.

In general terms, an artificial neural network can be seen as a method of approximation of an unknown function, which usually represents a complex nonlinear process. Moreover, there is a universal approximation theorem that shows that a neural network can approximate any continuous function for inputs within a specific range. However, a large-size network may lead to problems of overfitting: it may contain more parameters than those that can be justified by the data set, thus generating a model that fits too closely a particular set of data, and may therefore fail to fit additional data well or to predict future observations accurately. Overfitting may also increase the computational time unnecessarily.

Annex E Uncertainty, Dynamic Programming, and Stochastic Control

In Chapter 5, on artificial intelligence, we saw examples in which an artificial agent had to make decisions with perfect information or with almost zero information, and we mentioned that there are intermediate cases in which an agent partially knows its environment. Usually, that means that the agent has a stochastic model of its environment, and it must determine an optimal sequence of actions in order to achieve its goal. In other words, the agent faces a problem of decision-making under uncertainty.

The most common way to model that problem is as a Markov decision process, so named after mathematician Andrei Markov, who formalized it in the late nineteenth century. A Markov process is one in which a system moves from one state to another according to a probability that depends exclusively on the state in which the system previously was. Figure Annex E.1 shows a system that has only two states, A and B, and the probabilities of moving from state A to state B (0.4), staying in A (0.6), moving from B to A (0.9), or staying in B (0.1).

The probabilities of going from one state to another are usually represented by a transition matrix like the one in Table Annex E.1, which shows

Annexes

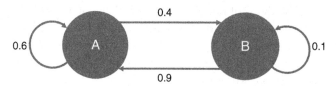

Figure Annex E.1 Markov process with two states and four transitions

the probabilities of moving from the state in each row to the states in each column, so the sum of the elements in each row is equal to one.

Table Annex E.1 *Transition probabilities of a Markov process with two states (A and B) and four transitions*

	A	B
A	0.6	0.4
B	0.9	0.1

A Markov decision process is an extension of a Markov process which adds actions and rewards. In a Markov decision process, an agent interacts with its stochastic environment through actions. Each action has a reward (or otherwise a cost) for the agent, and causes a transition from one state to another according to the transition probabilities matrix.

A Markov decision process is a stochastic control process. Stochastic control is a discipline that has its origins in mathematics and engineering, and that began to be incorporated in economics mainly from the 1960s and 1970s (Kendrick, 2005) thanks to the works of pioneers such as David A. Kendrick, Gregory Chow, Robert Pindyck, and others.

In a stochastic control problem an agent seeks to maximize the sum of rewards (or, alternatively, minimize the sum of costs) of its actions, given the stochastic behavior of the environment. To do this, it must find a policy, that is, a set of functions g_t that specifies what action a_t to take in each state s_t.

The problem may be specified for a finite or infinite time horizon. In the first case, we obtain a non-stationary solution (i.e., the optimal action in a state can change over time). In the second case, a stationary solution is obtained, where the optimal action depends only on the state, not the time.

In mathematical terms, for a finite horizon the problem can be expressed as finding a set of functions $g = \{g_0, \ldots, g_T\}$ such that $a_t = (s_t)$, in order to maximize the value of J, which is equal to the expected value of the sum of rewards for a finite sequence of t-periods, with terminal period T:

$$J = E\{\Sigma_{t=0}^{T}\delta^t R(s_t, a_t)\} \tag{E.1}$$

where E is the expected value operator that is taken over the transition probabilities $p_t^a(s_t, s_{t+1})$, that is, over the probabilities of moving from state s_t to state s_{t+1} when action a_t is taken; δ is a time discount factor that can take values between 0 and 1; and R is the reward of taking action a_t in state s_t.

The most common procedure for solving this problem is dynamic programming. In Chapter 5 we had an introduction to dynamic programming with a finite horizon, in a problem in which the agent knew its environment perfectly. Here we are no longer in a deterministic environment, but we are dealing with a stochastic one, in which the agent knows the states, rewards, and transition probabilities from one state to another, since these transitions are no longer known for sure.

The solution of the finite horizon problem is given, like that seen for the deterministic case in Chapter 5, by a backward recursive algorithm. From a terminal condition, the Bellman equation is applied to obtain the optimal value function V (also known as reward-to-go or, alternatively, as cost-to-go if the reward of the action is negative) which now, unlike the deterministic case, contains the E symbol, which as we said previously represents the expected value. The algorithm starts from the terminal condition:

$$V_T(s) = R_t(s) \tag{E.2}$$

and continues from back to front:

$$V_t(s) = \max\{R_t(s, a) + \delta\, E[V_{t+1}(s')]\} \qquad \text{for } t = T-1, T-2,\ldots, 0 \tag{E.3}$$

where s is the current state and s' is the next state. Once the iterations are finished, the optimal sequence of actions $a_t = g_t(s_t)$ is obtained, and also that V_0 equals the maximum value of J. For an infinite horizon, the problem can be expressed as maximizing the value of J for an infinite sequence of periods:

$$J = E\{\Sigma_{t=0}^{\infty}\delta^t R(s_t, a_t)\} \tag{E.4}$$

The solution to the problem is given by the following Bellman equation:

$$V(s) = \max\{R(s, a) + \delta E[V(s')]\} \tag{E.5}$$

This Bellman equation represents a system of equations, one for each state, and where the number of equations is equal to the number of V(.) unknowns. The presence of the max operator makes it a system of nonlinear equations, very difficult to solve analytically. There are two main methods or algorithms to solve the system, and thus computing an optimal policy: the value iteration method and the policy iteration method, that operate numerically by successive approximations.

When the transition probabilities from one state to another are not known, direct approximation methods can be applied, which are based on Monte Carlo simulations.[14] The direct approximation method for the value iteration method is temporal-difference learning, while that corresponding to the policy iteration method is Q-learning, of which we presented a simple example in Chapter 5 in Section 5.4 on reinforcement learning. In fact, temporal-difference learning and Q-learning are widely used in reinforcement learning, so that reinforcement learning can be thought of as the direct approximation to dynamic programming. These two fields developed independently for a long time: on the one hand, dynamic programming evolved mostly within operations research and control theory, and therefore through the use of classic methods rooted in applied mathematics; on the other hand, reinforcement learning did so within artificial intelligence, a field in which logic, discrete mathematics, computer science, and heuristics, are eclectically mixed. However, both fields are today very close to each other (Tsitsiklis, 2010).

When the number of states is large, dynamic programming suffers from what is known as the curse of dimensionality: the computational complexity of the problem grows exponentially with the number of states, which makes a problem with many states intractable with conventional solution methods and even with those of direct approximation. In such a case, indirect approximation methods can be applied, which aim not to obtain an optimal solution but, using Monte Carlo methods, toward the best possible approximation given the available resources. For linear approximations, the least-

---

[14] For details about the direct approximation methods, and for the indirect approximation methods mentioned in the following, see Haykin (2009), pp. 627–671.

squares policy evaluation method is used, while for nonlinear approaches, neural network-based methods are used.

Applications of dynamic programming and stochastic control methods in economics are numerous. For example, they can be applied to the case of a consumer who wants to determine the best intertemporal sequence of consumption and savings decisions, or to a firm that must determine an optimal sequence of investment decisions, or to the central bank of a country that wants to determine how best to carry out its monetary policy over time to control the evolution of the price level and/or that of gross domestic product.

In economic applications, it is common to mathematically state a stochastic control problem as one of maximizing the target function:

$$J = E\left\{\sum_{t=0}^{T-1} \delta^t F(x_t, u_t) + \delta^T W(x_T)\right\} \qquad (E.6)$$

subject, as a constraint, to the following dynamic equation:

$$x_{t+1} = H(x_t, u_t, \varepsilon_t) \qquad (E.7)$$

where J is the value function (or target function) to maximize, x is the state variable (analogous to the s variable we used earlier), u is the control variable (analogous to the action variable a we used earlier), ε is an identical and independently distributed stochastic shock, and where F, W, and H, are functions. The dynamic equation is a mathematical representation of the temporal evolution of some relevant economic variables. For example, the state variable x can be interpreted as the evolution of a consumer's wealth, and the control variable u can be interpreted as consumption level; or x can be the capital stock of a firm, and u its level of investment; or x can be the price level or gross domestic product of a country, and u the money supply controlled by the central bank.[15]

The dynamic programming solution for this problem is to find the value function $V(x_0)$ that gives the highest feasible expected value from the initial state, and the optimal control u as a function of the state x in each period. The value function that solves the problem satisfies the Bellman equation:

---

[15] We are exemplifying with simple models with one state and one control variable. But the models and results we will see can easily be generalized to the case of many state and control variables.

$$V_t(x_t) = \max_{u_t} \{F(x_t, u_t) + \delta E[V_{t+1}(x_{t+1})]\} \qquad (E.8)$$

with terminal condition:

$$V_T(x_t) = W(x_T) \qquad (E.9)$$

Particularly important for its analytical tractability, and with many applications, especially in the field of macroeconomic policy, are problems in which the objective function is quadratic and the dynamic equation is linear, called quadratic-linear problems.[16] In these problems, state and control variables often represent deviations from desired paths, so the goal it to minimize such deviations. The mathematical form of a quadratic-linear problem is specified as minimizing the objective function:

$$J = E\left\{\frac{1}{2}\delta^T w\ x_T^2 + \frac{1}{2}\sum_{t=0}^{T-1}\delta^t(w\ x_t^2 + \lambda\ u_t^2)\right\} \qquad (E.10)$$

subject to:

$$x_{t+1} = a\ x_t + b\ u_t + \varepsilon_t \qquad (E.11)$$

where x is the target variable, u the policy instrument,[17] and where w and λ are positive weights for the target variable and the policy instrument respectively, which indicate the relative value that the policymaker attaches to the deviations of such variables from its desired paths. Thanks to the linear-quadratic form of the problem, the dynamic programming solution is the feedback rule:

$$u_t = g_t\ x_t \qquad (E.12)$$

where g_t, called feedback gain coefficient in the stochastic control literature, is given by:

$$g_t = -(E\{\lambda + \delta\ k_{t+1}b^2\})^{-1}E\{\delta\ k_{t+1}\ a\ b\} \qquad (E.13)$$

---

[16] For comprehensive and in-depth presentations of stochastic control methods in economics, see Kendrick (1981) and Sengupta and Fanchon (1997). For macroeconomic applications with computational methods, see Kendrick, Mercado, and Amman (2006), part III.

[17] From what was said in the text, x and u can be interpreted as representing deviations from desired values.

where the evolution of k_t is given by the Riccati equations:

$$k_T = w \tag{E.14}$$

for the terminal period T, and:

$$k_t = E\{w + \delta k_{t+1}a^2\} - (E\{\lambda + \delta k_{t+1}b^2\})^{-1} (E\{\delta k_{t+1}ab\})^2 \tag{E.15}$$

for any other period. The Riccati equations are solved sequentially backwards, from the terminal period to the initial period. Note that despite being a stochastic problem with additive uncertainty (since the stochastic shock ε appears in that way in dynamic equation E.11), the solution does not contain any stochastic term. In fact, it is equivalent to solving the same problem without uncertainty, so it is said to display the certainty equivalence property. This equivalence is broken if we consider that the coefficients b and/or a from dynamic equation (E.11) are also uncertain (i.e., each has an associated variance). In this case, it is said that uncertainty is multiplicative, because these coefficients multiply the state and control variables respectively. This makes the expression of the feedback gain coefficient g_t more complex (Mercado and Kendrick, 2006).

There may also be uncertainty about the true model of the economy (i.e., as to the validity of the specification of the model being used) and therefore we may wish to take precautions in that regard, taking actions that are robust for a set of possible models that are supposed to be more or less close to the specified model. In such a case, we face what is known as a robust control problem, whose applications in economics and finance were pioneered by Lars Hansen, Berc Rustem, and Thomas Sargent. The starting point in a robust control problem is a nominal model of the form:

$$x_{t+1} = a\, x_t + b\, u_t + \varepsilon_t + z_t \tag{E.16}$$

where the z variable is a specification shock that is used to represent alternative models. The problem is posed as a zero-sum game between the controller (i.e., the one who manipulates the control variable) and "nature," where the controller tries to minimize the deviations in its objective function by optimally using the policy instrument u, while nature tries, malevolently, to maximize such deviations through z.[18]

---

[18] For a comprehensive and in-depth presentation of robust control in economics, see Hansen and Sargent (2007).

Finally, it is worth mentioning a very important type of stochastic control problem known as active learning. In this kind of problem, the controller has to dynamically solve a dual problem: learning from the system it is controlling (in other words, reducing the variance of the coefficients of the dynamic model that it wants to control) and at the same time minimizing deviations from the optimal path to achieve its objective. To achieve the first (increase its knowledge), it must explore the behavior of the system through random manipulations of the control variable, in order to generate multiple system responses and thereby increase the available information about its behavior. But to achieve the latter, it must exploit the information it already has and compute the optimal path of the control variable to reach its goal. Clearly, the controller faces a trade-off between exploring and exploiting. When exploring it may deviate from the optimal path of actions; when exploiting only the limited information it has may not yield the best possible performance. The essence of this type of problem is, then, to find the optimal sequence of actions that best combine the costs and benefits of exploring and exploiting.[19]

---

[19] For an introduction and a systematic outlook of active learning problems, see Kendrick, Amman, and Tucci (2014).

References

Albin, Peter (1992). Approximations of Cooperative Equilibria in Multi-Person Prisoner's Dilemma Played by Cellular Automata. *Mathematical Social Sciences*, 24 (2–3): pp. 293–319.

Albin, Peter (1998). *Barriers and Bounds to Rationality: Essays on Economic Complexity and Dynamics in Interactive Systems*. Princeton University Press, New Jersey.

Alchian, Armen (1950). Uncertainty, Evolution and Economic Theory. *Journal of Political Economy*, 58(3): 211–221.

Alpaydin, Ethem (2014). *Introduction to Machine Learning*. The MIT Press, Cambridge, MA.

Anderson, Phillip (1972). More Is Different. *Science*, 177(4047): 393–396.

Arrow, Kenneth and Frank Hahn (1983). *General Competitive Analysis*. North-Holland, Amsterdam.

Arthur, W. Brian (2014). *Complexity and the Economy*. Oxford University Press, New York.

Axelrod, Robert (1997). *The Complexity of Cooperation*. Princeton University Press, New Jersey.

Axtell, Robert (2000). Why Agents? For the Varied Motivations for Agent Computing in the Social Sciences. Working Paper 17, Center on Social and Economic Dynamics, The Brookings Institution, Washington DC.

Bailey, Kenneth (2006). Systems Theory. In Jonathan Turner (ed.), *Handbook of Sociological Theory*, pp. 379–401. Springer.

Becker, Gary (1962). Irrational Behavior and Economic Theory. *Journal of political Economy*, 70(1): 1–13.

Becker, Gary (1993). The Economic Way of Looking at Life. Working Paper 12, Coase-Sandor Institute for Law & Economics, Chicago.

Bermúdez, José (2014). *Cognitive Science: An Introduction to the Science of Mind*. Cambridge University Press, New York.

Blaug, Mark (1992). *The Methodology of Economics*. Cambridge University Press, Cambridge.

Boccara (2004). *Modeling Complex Systems*. Springer Verlag, New York.

Boero, Ricardo, Mateo Morini, Michele Sonessa and Pietro Terna (2015). *Agent-Based Models of the Economy: From Theory to Applications*. Palgrave MacMillan, Basingstoke, UK.

Borrill, Joseph and Leigh Tesfatsion (2010). Agent-Based Modeling: The Right Mathematics for the Social Sciences? Working Paper 10023, Department of Economics, Iowa State University, Iowa, USA.

Bourdieu, Pierre (1977). *Outline of a Theory of Practice*. Cambridge University Press, Cambridge.

Boyd, Robert and Peter Richerson (1985). *Culture and the Evolutionary Process*. University of Chicago Press, Chicago.

Bowles, Samuel (2003). *Microeconomics: Behavior, Institutions and Evolution*. Part III. Princeton University Press, New Jersey.

Brandstätter, Christian, Dietmar Dietrich, Klaus Doblhammer et al. (2015). *Natural Scientific, Psychoanalytical Model of the Psyche for Simulation and Emulation*. Scientific Report III, Institute of Computer Technology, Vienna University of Technology, Vienna.

Brenner, Thomas (2006). Agent Learning Representation: Advice on Modelling Economic Learning. In Tesfatsion Leigh and Kenneth Judd (eds.), *Handbook of Computational Economics, Vol. 2: Agent-Based Computational Economics*, pp. 894–947. North-Holland, Amsterdam.

Bridges, Douglas and Erik Palmgren (2018). Constructive Mathematics. In Edward N. Zalta (ed.), *The Stanford Encyclopedia of Philosophy* (Summer 2018 ed.), https://plato.stanford.edu/archives/sum2018/entries/mathematics-constructive.

Bridges, Douglas and Steve Reeves (1997). *Constructive Mathematics in Theory and Programming Practice, CDMTCS-068*, Centre For Discrete Mathematics and Theoretical Computer Science, University of Waikato, Auckland, NZ.

Brock, William and David Colander (2000). Complexity and Policy. In David Colander (ed.), *The Complexity Vision and the Teaching of Economics*, pp. 73–96. Edward Elgar, Cheltenham, UK.

Bucci, Wilma (1997). *Psychoanalysis & Cognitive Science: A Multiple Code Theory*. Guilford Press, New York.

Calvo, Paco and Toni Gomila (eds.) (2008). *Handbook of Cognitive Science: An Embodied Approach*. Elsevier Science & Technology, Oxford.

Camerer, Colin (2008). The Case for Mindful Economics. In Andrew Caplin and Andrew Schotter (eds.), *Foundations of Positive and Normative Economics: A Handbook*, pp. 43–69. Oxford University Press, New York.

Carley, Kathleen (2006). Computational Approaches to Sociological Theorizing. In Jonathan Turner (ed.), *Handbook of Sociological Theory*, pp. 69–83. Springer.

Cavalli-Sforza, Luigi Luca and Marcus Feldman (1981). *Cultural Transmission and Evolution: A Quantitative Approach*. Princeton University Press, New Jersey.

Chen, Shu-Heng (2012). Varieties of Agents in Agent-Based Computational Economics: A Historical and Interdisciplinary Perspective. *Journal of Economics Dynamics and Control*, 36(1): 1–25.

Chen, Shu-Heng (2016). *Agent-Based Computational Economics: How the Idea Originated and Where It Is Going*. Routledge, London.

Chenery, Hollis (1975). The Structuralist Approach to Development Policy. *American Economic Review*, 65(2): 310–316.

Chomsky, Noam (1959). A Review of B. F. Skinner's *Verbal Behavior*. *Language*, 35(1): 26–58.

Colander, David and Roland Kupers (2014). *Complexity and the Art of Public Policy: Solving Society's Problems from the Bottom Up*. Princeton University Press, New Jersey.

Cole, David (2020). The Chinese Room Argument. In Edward N. Zalta (ed.), *The Stanford Encyclopedia of Philosophy* (Spring 2020 ed.), https://plato.stanford.edu /archives/spr2020/entries/chinese-room/.

Crutchfield, James (1994). The Calculi of Emergence: Computation, Dynamics and Induction. *Physica D*, 75: 11–54.

Damaceanu, Romulus-Catalin (2013). *Agent-Based Computational Economics Using NetLogo*. Bentham Science Publishers, Sharjah, UAE.

Damasio, Antonio (2005). *Descartes's Error*. Penguin Books, New York.

Damasio, Antonio (2009). Neuroscience and the Emergence of Neuroeconomics. In Paul Glimcher (ed.), *Neuroeconomics: Decisionmaking and The Brain*, pp. 209–214. Elsevier Science Publishing, San Diego.

Dawid, Herbert and Andreas Pyka (2018). Special Issue on Evolutionary Dynamics and Agent-Based Modeling. *Computational Economics*, 52(3).

Dawkins, Richard (2006). *The Selfish Gene*. 30th anniversary ed. Oxford University Press, Oxford.

Debreu, Gerard (1972). *Theory of Value: An Axiomatic Analysis of Economic Equilibrium*. Yale University Press, New Haven.

Delli Gatti, Domenico, Georgio Fagiolo, Mauro Gallegati, Matteo Riciardi and Alberto Russo (eds.) (2018). *Agent-Based Models in Economics: A Toolkit*. Cambridge University Press, Cambridge.

Dennett, Daniel (1996). *Darwin's Dangerous Idea: Evolution and the Meanings of Life*. Penguin Books, London.

Dietrich, Dietmar, Georg Fodor, Gerhard Zucker and Dietmar Bruckner (eds.) (2009). *Simulating the Mind: A Technical Neuropsychoanalytical Approach*. Springer-Verlag, Vienna.

Dietrich, Franz and Christian List (2016). Mentalism versus Behaviorism in Economics: A Philosophy of Science Perspective. *Economics & Philosophy*, (32)2: 249–281.

Dreyfus, Hubert (1972). *What Computers Can't Do: A Critique of Artificial Reason*. Harper & Row, New York.

Dreyfus, Hubert (1992). *What Computer's Still Can't Do*. The MIT Press, Cambridge, MA.

Durlauf, Steven (2012). Complexity, Economics and Public Policy. *Politics, Philosophy & Economics*, 11(1): 45–75.

Ehrentreich, Norman (2008). *Agent-Based Modeling: The Santa Fe Institute Artificial Stock Market Revisited*, Part II. Springer-Verlag, Berlin.

Elsenbroich, Corinna and Nigel Gilbert (2013). *Modelling Norms*. Springer, Dordrecht.

Epstein, Joshua (2006). *Generative Social Science: Studies in Agent-Based Computational Modeling*. Princeton University Press, New Jersey.

Epstein, Joshua (2013). *Agent_Zero: Toward Neurocognitive Foundations for Generative Social Science*. Princeton University Press, New Jersey.

Epstein, Joshua and Robert Axtell (1996). *Growing Artificial Societies: Social Science from the Bottom Up*. The MIT Press, Cambridge MA.

Fine, Ben and Dimitri Milonakys (2009). *From Economics Imperialism to Freakonomics*. Routledge, London.

Flache, Andreas and Rainer Hegselmann (1998). Understanding Complex Social Dynamics: A Plea for Cellular Automata Based Modelling. *Journal of Artificial Societies and Social Simulation*, 1(3).

Frankish, Keith and William Ramsey (eds.) (2012). *The Cambridge Handbook of Cognitive Science*. Cambridge University Press, Cambridge.

Franks, David (2019). *Neurosociology: Fundamentals and Current Findings*. Springer, Dordrecht.

Franks, David and Jonathan Turner (2013). *Handbook of Neurosociology*. Springer, Dordrecht.

Friedenberg, Jay and Gordon Silverman (2011). *Cognitive Science: and introduction to the study of mind*. SAGE Publications, Inc.

Friedman, Milton (1966). The Methodology of Positive Economics. In Milton Friedman (ed.), *Essays in Positive Economics*, pp. 3–16 and pp. 30–43. University of Chicago Press, Chicago.

Fudenberg, Drew and Jean Tirole (1991). *Game Theory*. The MIT Press, Cambridge, MA.

Gelbard, Friedrich (2017). *Psychoanalytic Defense Mechanisms in Cognitive Multi-Agent Systems*. Routledge, London.

Gershenson, Carlos and Nelson Fernández (2012). Complexity and Information: Measuring Emergence, Self-Organization and Homeostasis at Multiple Scales. *Complexity*, 18(2): 29–44.

Giddens, Anthony (1986). *The Constitution of Society: Outline of the Theory of Structuration*. Polity Press, Oxford.

Gilbert, Nigel (2019). *Agent-Based Models*. SAGE Publications, Thousand Oaks, CA.

Gintis, Herbert (2009). *Game Theory Evolving*. Princeton University Press, New Jersey.

Glimcher, Paul (2003). *Decisions, Uncertainty and the Brain: The Science of Neuroeconomics*. The MIT Press, Cambridge, MA.

Glimcher, Paul and Ernst Fehr (2014). *Neuroeconomics: Decision Making and the Brain*. 2nd ed. Elsevier Science Publishing, San Diego.

Gode, Dhananjay and Shyam Sunder (1993). Allocative Efficiency of Markets with Zero-Intelligence Traders: Market as a Partial Substitute for Individual Rationality. *Journal of Political Economy*, 101(1): 119–137.

Goodfellow, Ian, Yoshua Bengio and Aaron Courville (2016). *Deep Learning*. The MIT Press, Cambridge, MA.

Gul, Faruk and Wolfang Pesendorfer (2008). The Case for Mindless Economics. In Andrew Caplin and Andrew Schotter (eds.), *Foundations of Positive and Normative Economics: A Handbook*, pp. 3–39. Oxford University Press, New York.

Hadeler, Karl-Peter and Johannes Müller (2017). *Cellular Automata: Analysis and Applications*. Springer International Publishing, Cham, Switzerland.

Hamill, Lynne and Nigel Gilbert (2016). *Agent-Based Modelling in Economics*. Wiley, West Sussex, UK.

Hansen, Lars and Thomas Sargent (2007). *Robustness*. Princeton University Press, New Jersey.

Harari, Yuval (2017). *Homo Deus: A Brief History of Tomorrow*. Vintage, London.

Hausman, Daniel (1992). *The Inexact and Separate Science of Economics*. The MIT Press, Cambridge, MA.

Hayek, Friedrich (1937). Economics and Knowledge. *Economica*, 4(13): 33–54.

Hayek, Friedrich (1945). The Use of Knowledge in Society. *The American Economic Review*, 35(4): 519–530.

Haykin, Simon (2009). *Neural Networks and Learning Machines*. Pearson, New Jersey.

Heidegger, Martin (2008). *Being and Time*. HarperCollins, New York.

Hicks, John and R. G. D. Allen (1934). A Reconsideration of the Theory of Value. *Economica*, Part I 1(1): 52–76 and Part II 1(1): 196–219.

Him, Xuewei, Jinpei Wu and Xueyan Li (2018). *Theory of Practical Cellular Automaton*. Beijing Jiaotong University Press and Springer Nature, Singapore.

Hodgson, Geoffrey (2004). Thorstein Veblen and Darwinism. *International Review of Sociology*, 14(3): 343–361.

Hollander, Christopher and Annie Wu (2011). The Current State of Normative Agent-Based Systems. *Journal of Artificial Societies and Social Simulation*, 14(2): 6.

Holt, Richard, J., Barkley Rosser Jr. and David Colander (2010). The Complexity Era in Economics. *Middlebury College Economics Discussion Paper*, 10–01, Middlebury, VT.

Hommes, Cars and Blake LeBaron (eds.) (2018). *Handbook of Computational Economics Vol. 4: Heterogeneous Agent Modeling*. North-Holland, Amsterdam.

Horgan, John (1995). From Complexity to Perplexity. *Scientific American*, 272(6): 104–120.

Horgan, John (2015). *The End of Science: Facing the Limits of Knowledge in the Twilight of the Scientific Age*, pp. 195–232. Basic Books, New York.

Huys, Quentin, Tiago Maia and Michael Frank (2016). Computational Psychiatry as a Bridge from Neuroscience to Clinical Applications. *Nature Neuroscience*, 19(3): 404–413.

Izquierdo, Luis, Segismundo Izquierdo, Joseph Galan and José Santos (2013). Combining Mathematical and Simulation Approaches to Understand the Dynamics of Computer Models. In Bruce Edmonds and Ruth Meyer (eds.), *Simulating Social Complexity*, pp. 293–330. Springer-Verlag, Berlin.

Kandel, Eric (2005). *Psychiatry, Psychoanalysis and the New Biology of Mind*. American Psychiatry Association Publishing, Virginia, USA.

Keenan, Donald and Mike O'Brien (1993). Competition, Collusion and Chaos. *Journal of Economic Dynamics and Control*, 17(3): 327–353.

Kendrick, David A. (1981). *Stochastic Control for Economic Models*. McGraw-Hill, New York.

Kendrick, David A. (2005). Stochastic Control for Economic Models: Past, Present and Paths Ahead. *Journal of Economic Dynamics and Control*, 29(1–2): 3–30.

Kendrick, David A., Hans Amman and Marco Tucci (2014). Learning About Learning. In Karl Schmedderss and Kenneth Judd (eds.), *Handbook of Computational Economics*, Vol. III, pp. 1–35. North-Holland, Amsterdam.

Kendrick, David A., Ruben Mercado and Hans Amman (2006). *Computational Economics*. Princeton University Press, Princeton, NJ.

Kirk, Robert (2019). Zombies. In Edward N. Zalta (ed.), *The Stanford Encyclopedia of Philosophy* (Spring 2019 ed.), https://plato.stanford.edu/archives/spr2019/entries/zombies/.

Lange, Oskar (1965). *Whole and Parts: A General Theory of Systems Behavior*. Pergamon Press, Oxford.

Laver, Michael (2020). *Agent-Based Models of Social Life: Fundamentals*. Cambridge University Press, Cambridge.

LeBaron, Blake (2002). Building the Santa Fe Artificial Stock Market. Working Paper, Brandeis University, Waltham MA, June.

Lefevre, Henry (2009). *Dialectical Materialism*, Part II. University of Minnesota Press, Minneapolis.

Leontief, Wassily (1941). *The Structure of American Economy 1919–1929*. Harvard University Press, Cambridge, MA.

Li, Xuewei, Jinpei Wu and Xueyan Li (2018). *Theory of Practical Cellular Automaton*. Springer Verlag, Singapore.

Lowe, Edward Jonathan (2000). *An Introduction to the Philosophy of Mind*. Cambridge University Press, Cambridge.

Martin-Löf, Per (1984). Constructive Mathematics and Computer Programming. *Philosophical Transactions of the Royal Society of London*, A312: 501–518.

Massey, Douglass (2002). A Brief History of Human Society: The Origin and Role of Emotion in Social Life. *American Sociological Review*, 67(1): 1–29.

Maynard Smith, John (1982). *Evolution and the Theory of Games*. Cambridge University Press, Cambridge.

Mercado, Ruben and David A. Kendrick (2006). Parameter Uncertainty and Policy Intensity: Some Extensions and Suggestions for Further Work. *Computational Economics*, 27: 483–496.

Miller, John and Scott Page (2007). *Complex Adaptive Systems: An Introduction to Computational Models of Social Life*. Princeton University Press, Princeton, NJ.

Mitchell, Melanie (1996). *An Introduction to Genetic Algorithms*. The MIT Press, Cambridge, MA.

Mitchell, Melanie (2009). *Complexity: A Guided Tour*. Oxford University Press, New York.

Newmann, Martin (2008). Homo Socionicus: A Case Study of Simulation Models of Norms. *Journal of Artificial Societies and Social Simulation*, 11(4).

Norman, Greg, Louise Hawkley, Maike Luhmann, John Cacioppo and Gary Berntson (2013). Social Neuroscience and the Modern Synthesis of Social and Biological Levels of Analysis. In Davis Franks and Jonathan Turner (eds.), *Handbook of Neurosociology*, pp. 67–81. Springer, Dordrecht.

Nowak, Martin and Robert May (1992). Evolutionary Games and Spatial Chaos. *Nature*, 359: 826–829.

Nowak, Martin and Robert May (1993). The Spatial Dilemmas of Evolution. *International Journal of Bifurcation and Chaos*, 3(1): 35–78.

O'Sullivan, David and Mordechai Haklay (2000). Agent-Based Models and Individualism: Is the World Agent-Based? *Environment and Planning A*, 32(8): 1409–1425.

Packard, Norman (1989). Intrinsic Adaptation in a Simple Model for Evolution. In Christopher Langton (ed.), *Artificial Life*, pp. 141–155. Addison-Wesley, Redwood City, CA.

Pigliucci, Massimo (2004). Between Holism and Reductionism: A Philosophical Primer on Emergence. *Biological Journal of the Linnean Society*, 112(2): 261–267.

Pinker, Steven (2002). *The Blank Slate: The Modern Denial of Human Nature*. Penguin Books, London.

Poole, David and Alan Mackworth (2017). *Artificial Intelligence: Foundations of Computational Agents*. Cambridge University Press, Cambridge.

Prawitz, Dag (1990). Tacit Knowledge: An Impediment for AI? In Bo Goranson and Magnus Florin (eds.), *Artificial Intelligence, Culture and Language: On Education and Work*, pp. 57–60. Springer-Verlag, London.

Railsback, Steven and Volker Grimm (2019). *Agent-Based and Individual-Based Modeling: A Practical Introduction*. 2nd ed. Princeton University Press, New Jersey.

Rangel, Antonio, Colin Camerer and P. Read Montague (2008). A Framework for Studying the Neurobiology of Value-Based Decision Making. *Nature Reviews Neuroscience*, 9(7): 45–56.

Ranish, Robert and Stefan Sorgner (2014). *Post and Transhumanism: An Introduction*. Peter Lang, Bern.

Rodado, Juan and Mario Rendon (1996). Can Psychoanalysis be of Help to Artificial Intelligence ... or ... Vice Versa? *The American Journal of Psychoanalysis*, 56: 395–413.

Rosser, J. Barkley Jr. (1999). On the Complexities of Complex Economic Dynamics. *Journal of Economic Perspectives*, 13(4): 169–192.

Rosser, J. Barkley Jr. (2015). Complexity and the Austrians. In Christopher Coyne and Peter Boettke (eds.), *The Oxford Handbook of Austrian Economics*, pp. 594–611. Oxford University Press, Oxford.

Roughgarden, Tim (2010). Computing Equilibria: A Computational Complexity Perspective. *Economic Theory*, 42: 193–236.

Russell, Stuart and Peter Norvig (2018). *Artificial Intelligence: A Modern Approach*. Pearson, Harlow UK.

Samuelson, Paul (1938). A Note on the Pure Theory of Consumers' Behaviour. *Economica*, 5(17): 61–71.

Sanderson, Stephen (2006). Evolutionary Theorizing. In Jonathan Turner (ed.), *Handbook of Sociological Theory*, pp. 435–455. Springer, New York.

Sandler, Joseph, Alex Holder, Christopher Dare and Anna Dreher (1997). *Freud's Models of the Mind: An Introduction*. Routledge, London.

Saygin, Ayse, Ilyas Cicekli and Varol Akman (2000). Turing Test: 50 Years Later. *Minds and Machines*, 10: 463–518.

Schatzki, Theodore (1996). *Social Practices: A Wittgensteinian Approach to Human Activity and the Social*. Cambridge University Press, Cambridge.

Schatzki, Theodore (2002). *The Site of the Social: A Philosophical Account of the Constitution of Social Life and Change*. Penn State University Press, University Park, PA.

Schumpeter, Joseph (1983). *The Theory of Economic Development*. Taylor & Francis, Somerset, UK.

Sengupta, Jati and Phillipe Fanchon (1997). *Control Theory Methods in Economics*. Springer-Verlag, New York.

Skinner, Burrhus F. (1957). *Verbal Behavior*. Appleton-Century-Crofts, New York.

Solms, Mark and Oliver Turnbull (2011). What Is Neuropsychoanalysis? *Neuropsychoanalysis*, 13(2): 133–145.

Squazzoni, Flaminio (2012). *Agent-Based Computational Sociology*. John Wiley & Sons, West Sussex, UK.

Sraffa, Piero (1960). *Production of Commodities by Means of Commodities: Prelude to a Critique of Economic Theory*. Cambridge University Press, London.

Standish, Russell (2008). Concept and Definition of Complexity. In Ang Yang and Yin Shan (eds.), *Intelligent Complex Adaptive Systems*, pp. 105–124. IGI Publishing, Hershey, PA.

Stets, Jan and Jonathan Turner (eds.) (2006). *Handbook of the Sociology of Emotions*. Springer-Verlag, New York.

Stigler, George (1984). Economics: The Imperial Science? *Scandinavian Journal of Economics*, 86(3): 301–313.

Sun, Ron (ed.) (2008). *The Cambridge Handbook of Computational Psychology*. Cambridge University Press, Cambridge.

Sutton, Richard and Andrew Barto (2018). *Reinforcement Learning: An Introduction*. 2nd ed. The MIT Press, Cambridge MA.

Taylor, Charles (1995). *Philosophical Arguments*, pp. 61–78. Harvard University Press, Cambridge MA.

Tesfatsion, Leigh and Kenneth Judd (eds.) (2006). *Handbook of Computational Economics. Vol. 2: Agent-Based Computational Economics*, North-Holland, Amsterdam.

Thagard, Paul (2005). *Mind: Introduction to Cognitive Science*. The MIT Press, Cambridge MA.

Thagard, Paul (2012). Cognitive Architectures. In Keith Frankish and William Ramsey (eds.), *The Cambridge Handbook of Cognitive Science*, pp. 50–70. Cambridge University Press, Cambridge.

Tomasello, Michael (2014). *A Natural History of Human Thinking*. Harvard University Press, Cambridge MA.

Tsitsiklis, John (2010). Commentary: Perspectives on Stochastic Optimization Over Time. *INFORMS Journal on Computing*, 22(1): 18–19.

Turing, Alan (1937). On Computable Numbers, with an Application to the Entscheidungsproblem. *Proceedings of the London Mathematical Society*, s2-42 (1): 230–265.

Turing, Alan (1950). Computing Machinery and Intelligence. *Mind*, 59(236): 433–460.

Turkle, Sherry (1988). Artificial Intelligence and Psychoanalysis: A New Alliance. *Daedalus*, (117)1: 241–268.

Turner, Jonathan (1986). The Theory of Structuration. *American Journal of Sociology*, 91(4): 969–977.

Turner, Jonathan and Alexandra Maryanski (2013). The Evolution of the Neurological Basis of Human Sociality. In David Franks and Jonathan Turner (eds.), *Handbook of Neurosociology*, pp. 289–309. Springer, Dordrecht.

Turner, Stephen (1994). *The Social Theory of Practices: Tradition, Tacit Knowledge, and Presuppositions*. The University of Chicago Press, Chicago.

Turner, Stephen (2015). *Understanding the Tacit*. Routledge, London.

Tye, Michael (2018). Qualia. In Edward N. Zalta (ed.), *The Stanford Encyclopedia of Philosophy* (Summer 2018 ed.), https://plato.stanford.edu/archives/sum2018/entries/qualia/.

van Nuys, David (2010). *An Interview with Wilma Bucci on Psychoanalysis and Cognitive Science*, Gulf Bend Center, Victoria, TX. Accessed November 10, 2020, www.gulfbend.org/poc/view_doc.php?type=doc&id=38296.

van Veen, Fjodor (2017). *The Neural Network Zoo*. The Asimov Institute, Utrecht. Accessed November 10, 2020, www.asimovinstitute.org/neural-network-zoo/.

Velupillai, K. Vela (2005). The Impossibility of an Effective Theory of Policy in a Complex Economy. Universita degli Study di Trento, Dipartimento di Economia, Discussion Paper 14.

Velupillai, K. Vela, Stefano Zambelli and Stephen Kinsella (eds.) (2012). *Computable Economics*. Edward Elgar Publishing, Cheltenham, UK.

Villatoro, Daniel, Giulia Andrighetto, Rosaria Conte and Jordi Sabater-Mir (2015). Self-Policing Through Norm Internalization: A Cognitive Solution to the Tragedy of the Digital Commons in Social Networks. *Journal of Artificial Societies and Social Simulation*, 18(2)2.

von Bertalannfy, Ludwig (2015). *General Systems Theory: Foundations, Development, Applications*. George Braziller, New York.

von Neumann, John (1951). The General and Logical Theory of Automata. In Lloyd Jeffress (ed.). *Cerebral Mechanisms in Behavior: The Hixon Symposium*, pp. 1–31. John Wiley & Sons, New York.

von Neumann, John (1958). *The Computer and the Brain*. Yale University Press, New Haven.

von Neumann, John and Oskar Morgenstern (2007). *Theory of Games and Economic Behavior*. Princeton University Press, New Jersey.

Walsh, Anthony (2014). *Biosociology: Bridging the Biology-Sociology Divide*, Routledge, London.

Weinberg, Stephen (1993). *Dreams of a Final Theory: The Search for the Fundamental Laws of Nature*, pp. 51–64. Vintage, New York.

Wilensky, Uri and William Rand (2015). *Introduction to Agent-Based Modeling: Modeling Natural, Social and Engineered Complex Systems with NetLogo*. The MIT Press, Cambridge, MA.

Wilson, Edward (1975). *Sociobiology: The New Synthesis*. Harvard University Press, Cambridge, MA.

Wilson, Edward (1978). *On Human Nature*. Harvard University Press, Cambridge, MA.

Wilson, Robert and Frank Keil (eds.) (2001). *The MIT Encyclopedia of the Cognitive Sciences*. The MIT Press, Cambridge MA.

Wittgenstein, Ludwig (2016). *Philosophical Investigations*. Wiley-Blackwell, Chichester, UK.

Wolfram, Stephen (2002). *A New Kind of Science*. Wolfram Media, Champaign, USA.

Zambelli, Stefano (2012). Computable Economics: Reconstructing the Nonconstructive. *New Mathematics and Natural Computation*, 8(1): 113–122.

Index

Printed in the United States
by Baker & Taylor Publisher Services